Troubleshooting Puppet

Troubleshoot your Puppet infrastructure to fix
problems quickly

Thomas Uphill

BIRMINGHAM - MUMBAI

Troubleshooting Puppet

First published: August 2015

Production reference: 1260815

Published by Packt Publishing Ltd.
Livery Place
35 Livery Street
Birmingham B3 2PB, UK.

ISBN 978-1-78439-865-1

www.packtpub.com

Credits

Author
Thomas Uphill

Reviewer
Fuat Ulugay

Commissioning Editor
Pramila Balan

Acquisition Editor
Subho Gupta

Content Development Editor
Anand Singh

Technical Editor
Siddhi Rane

Copy Editor
Vedangi Narvekar

Project Coordinator
Vijay Kushlani

Proofreader
Safis Editing

Indexer
Hemangini Bari

Production Coordinator
Nitesh Thakur

Cover Work
Nitesh Thakur

About the Author

Thomas Uphill is an RHCA who has been using Puppet since version 0.24.
He has been a system administrator for nearly 20 years, more than 10 of which
have been with Red Hat Linux and its derivatives. He wrote *Mastering Puppet*,
Packt Publishing, a book on deploying Puppet in an Enterprise setting. He enjoys
teaching others how to use Puppet to automate as much as possible. He runs the
Seattle Puppet Users Group (PUGS) and volunteers with LOPSA and SASAG.
You can find him at `http://ramblings.narrabilis.com`.

I would like to thank my wife, Priya Fernandes, for her support
while writing this book. Thank you to my PUGS members and
Puppet Labs for troubleshooting problems and suggestions. Thank
you to Andrew Parker for his input and support. Thank you to
my reviewers and the support staff at Packt Publishing. And I'm
thankful to everyone who bought *Mastering Puppet* and made it
possible for me to write this book.

About the Reviewer

Fuat Ulugay is currently the IT and ERP director for SOCAR Turkey. He lives in Istanbul, Turkey. He also worked as an SAP ABAP and CRM consultant for 17 years.

He is a great fan of open source projects. He implements and teaches them whenever possible. He is good at penetration testing, network security monitoring, industrial control systems security, system administration, and virtualization. He is also leading and teaching the security team at his company. He has a blog, `http:/hacktr.org`, where he writes about open source and security-related topics. He wrote the book *Learning Puppet for Windows Server* for Packt Publishing.

www.PacktPub.com

Support files, eBooks, discount offers, and more

For support files and downloads related to your book, please visit
www.PacktPub.com.

Did you know that Packt offers eBook versions of every book published, with PDF
and ePub files available? You can upgrade to the eBook version at www.PacktPub.
com and as a print book customer, you are entitled to a discount on the eBook copy.
Get in touch with us at service@packtpub.com for more details.

At www.PacktPub.com, you can also read a collection of free technical articles,
sign up for a range of free newsletters and receive exclusive discounts and offers
on Packt books and eBooks.

https://www2.packtpub.com/books/subscription/packtlib

Do you need instant solutions to your IT questions? PacktLib is Packt's online digital
book library. Here, you can search, access, and read Packt's entire library of books.

Why subscribe?

- Fully searchable across every book published by Packt
- Copy and paste, print, and bookmark content
- On demand and accessible via a web browser

Free access for Packt account holders

If you have an account with Packt at www.PacktPub.com, you can use this to access
PacktLib today and view 9 entirely free books. Simply use your login credentials for
immediate access.

Table of Contents

Preface

Puppet is a configuration management system that was written for system administrators so that they could manage a large number of systems efficiently and help maintain order. The deployment of Puppet becomes more complex as you increase the number of nodes in your environment. This book will help you troubleshoot your Puppet infrastructure to leverage your system's performance effectively by using different methods and techniques.

What this book covers

Chapter 1, *Puppet Infrastructure*, introduces the various components of a Puppet installation. We cover the problems that arise in the infrastructure and communication between the components.

Chapter 2, *Writing Puppet Manifests*, talks about manifests—the files in which you write the Puppet code. We look at some Puppet code, the common syntax, and formatting problems. We examine tools to help correct our code and discover how to use Git to automatically check our manifests. We also look at a few popular editors and how to configure them to help us edit Puppet code.

Chapter 3, *Modules and Templates*, looks at how code is organized in modules. We'll cover the non-manifest code that is also present in modules such as custom facts. We'll also look at templates and how to debug issues with them.

Chapter 4, *Hiera and External Node Classifiers*, is about Hiera, a hierarchical *key:value* lookup tool that helps Puppet keep the code and data distinct. An external node classifier (ENC) is a way of determining the classes that are applied to a node. In this chapter, we look at the problems that occur when configuring and using these tools.

Chapter 5, The Marionette Collective, examines MCollective, a Puppet Labs orchestration tool. ActiveMQ is the message broker that is used by MCollective. We cover problems with the configuration of both ActiveMQ and MCollective.

Chapter 6, PuppetDB and Puppet Server, describes how both these tools were written to deal with problems concerning scale. PuppetDB deals with exported resources and reporting and utilizes PostgreSQL. Puppet Server uses the TrapperKeeper framework that was developed by Puppet Labs and relies on a JVM and JRuby. In this chapter, we explore the problems with these tools and how to debug them using Ruby tools.

Chapter 7, Help Me!, looks at where you can go when you need some help. We introduce many of the community resources that are available to you when you cannot solve your Puppet problems.

What you need for this book

This book requires a Puppet installation—either the open source version or Puppet Enterprise. The material covers versions later than Version 3, which includes Version 4. You will need some test nodes with which you can experiment.

Who this book is for

This book is for moderate to advanced Puppet engineers who work with Puppet in a production environment. The book aims to solve real-world problems that occur in real deployments.

Conventions

In this book, you will find a number of text styles that distinguish between different kinds of information. Here are some examples of these styles and an explanation of their meaning.

Code words in text, database table names, folder names, filenames, file extensions, pathnames, dummy URLs, user input, and Twitter handles are shown as follows: "Puppet Labs suggested that hook runs `puppet parser validate` against all the files ending in the `.pp` extension."

A block of code is set as follows:

```
<root level="debug">
<!--<appender-ref ref="STDOUT"/>-->
<appender-ref ref="${logappender:-DUMMY}" />
```

```
<appender-ref ref="F1"/>
</root>
```

When we wish to draw your attention to a particular part of a code block, the relevant lines or items are set in bold:

```
<root level="debug">
<!--<appender-ref ref="STDOUT"/>-->
<appender-ref ref="${logappender:-DUMMY}" />
<appender-ref ref="F1"/>
</root>
```

Any command-line input or output is written as follows:

```
$ openssl verify -CAfile ca_crt.pem mylaptop.pem
mylaptop.pem: OK
```

New terms and **important words** are shown in bold. Words that you see on the screen, for example, in menus or dialog boxes, appear in the text like this: "Once your project is imported, apply the Puppet nature to the project by selecting the **Add Puppet Nature** option."

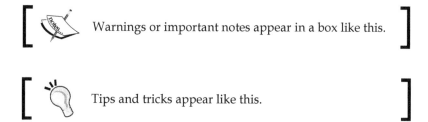

Warnings or important notes appear in a box like this.

Tips and tricks appear like this.

Reader feedback

Feedback from our readers is always welcome. Let us know what you think about this book—what you liked or disliked. Reader feedback is important for us as it helps us develop titles that you will really get the most out of.

To send us general feedback, simply e-mail feedback@packtpub.com, and mention the book's title in the subject of your message.

If there is a topic that you have expertise in and you are interested in either writing or contributing to a book, see our author guide at www.packtpub.com/authors.

Customer support

Now that you are the proud owner of a Packt book, we have a number of things to help you to get the most from your purchase.

Errata

Although we have taken every care to ensure the accuracy of our content, mistakes do happen. If you find a mistake in one of our books—maybe a mistake in the text or the code—we would be grateful if you could report this to us. By doing so, you can save other readers from frustration and help us improve subsequent versions of this book. If you find any errata, please report them by visiting http://www.packtpub.com/submit-errata, selecting your book, clicking on the **Errata Submission Form** link, and entering the details of your errata. Once your errata are verified, your submission will be accepted and the errata will be uploaded to our website or added to any list of existing errata under the Errata section of that title.

To view the previously submitted errata, go to https://www.packtpub.com/books/content/support and enter the name of the book in the search field. The required information will appear under the **Errata** section.

Piracy

Piracy of copyrighted material on the Internet is an ongoing problem across all media. At Packt, we take the protection of our copyright and licenses very seriously. If you come across any illegal copies of our works in any form on the Internet, please provide us with the location address or website name immediately so that we can pursue a remedy.

Please contact us at copyright@packtpub.com with a link to the suspected pirated material.

We appreciate your help in protecting our authors and our ability to bring you valuable content.

Questions

If you have a problem with any aspect of this book, you can contact us at questions@packtpub.com, and we will do our best to address the problem.

1
Puppet Infrastructure

As a Puppet engineer, you will encounter many different problems while working with Puppet. Puppet infrastructure comprises all the components that you can use to deploy Puppet on your nodes, and may include applications such as Apache, Passenger, Puppet Server, PuppetDB, and ActiveMQ. Knowing how the infrastructure works, and how the various components fit together and function, will help you troubleshoot your issues. An important aspect of how Puppet infrastructure works is the way the various components communicate with each other. Most of the communication between the components of your Puppet infrastructure is done via an HTTP/SSL REST API. Later in this chapter, we will use this API to troubleshoot our installation.

The first step towards understanding how all the components of a Puppet installation communicate is to know the different components. The components of a typical installation are shown in the following diagram:

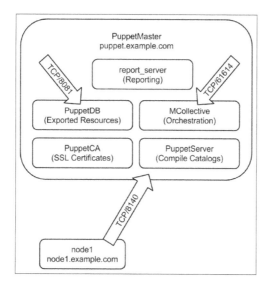

In subsequent chapters, we will examine the workings of these various components in detail.

With this picture of the components in mind, we will now go through the main actions that take place during a Puppet run.

The lifecycle of a Puppet run

Communication between the nodes and the master in a Puppet environment is verified with a system of X.509 SSL certificates. The master operates as a **certificate authority (CA)** for the system, although you may specify another server to act as the CA. When the agent first runs on a node, there are several steps taken to set up the trust relationship between the node and the master, which are outlined as follows:

1. The agent contacts the master and downloads the CA certificate.

2. The agent generates a certificate for itself based on the `certname` configuration option, which is usually equivalent to the hostname of the node.

3. The agent issues a **certificate signing request (CSR)** to the master, asking the master to sign its certificate.

4. The master may choose to sign the certificate (if automatic signing is configured) or the operator of the master may sign the certificate.

5. The agent will check back every 2 minutes by default (configurable with the `waitforcert` option) to check whether its certificate has been signed.

6. Once it has been signed, the agent will download its signed certificate.

At this point, the trust relationship between the agent and master has been established. The subsequent Puppet runs will not have to perform these steps. These runs will have a different series of steps, which are outlined in the following list:

1. The agent contacts and informs the master about its operating environment. Environments are used to separate nodes into logical groups.

2. The master looks through all the available modules in the given environment and begins sending all the `/lib` subdirectories of the modules to the agent via the `pluginsync` method.

3. Once all the plugins have been downloaded to the node, the node runs the `facter` utility to generate a list of facts about the node. The agent then ships the fact list back to the master.

4. If you have PuppetDB configured in your environment, the facts are shipped to PuppetDB, which will decide to either create new entries for the node (if this is the first time, facts have arrived for this node), or update the existing fact values.

5. At this point, the master will use the fact list to generate values that are needed to compile the **catalog** for the node. A catalog is the living document of how a node is configured. It consists of all the Puppet modules, classes, and resources, that will be applied to a node.

6. The master will compile the catalog. This is the process of verifying that it is possible to apply resources to a node in a consistent manner. Puppet will generate a graph, with all the resources as vertices. If the graph has any cycles, then the compilation will fail. A cycle is also known as a circular dependency. It means that there are resources within the catalog that require each other, or that are mutually dependent. A failed compilation results in the agent exiting with an error code.

7. If the catalog compiles successfully, the catalog is then shipped to the agent.

8. At this point, the Puppet agent's run begins. All the resources in the catalog are applied sequentially to the node. When troubleshooting, it is important to remember that although the master is capable of running several catalog compilations at once, the agent on a node must be single-threaded by definition.

9. The catalog will either apply without error to the node, which is called a **clean run**, or fail and output errors. If the agent has a clean run and does not change any files on the node, the exit code of the process will be 0. If the agent has a clean run and does make any changes, the exit code will be 2. If the agent fails to apply all the resources to the node, which is called a **failed run**, the agent will exit with the exit code as either 4 (with no file changes) or 6 (with file changes).

 To have puppet agent return these exit codes, the --detailed-exitcodes option must be given when running the puppet agent. Note the test option, -t, includes this option.

10. Facter will be run at the end of a successful or clean run. The fact values that have changed or the new facts will be sent to PuppetDB. Note that if PuppetDB cannot be updated, the agent will mark the run as unclean.

11. Depending on your configuration, the agent will then generate a report, which will be shipped to the report_server. If reports are configured, then they will be sent for both failed and clean runs.

12. Several files on the node will also be updated at this point. When troubleshooting, it is often useful to examine the contents of the following files:

- The `classes.txt` file contains the list of classes in the catalog
- The `resources.txt` file contains a list of resources in the catalog
- The `state.yaml` file contains timestamps for various files on the system as well as scheduling information
- The `last_run_report.yaml` file contains all the log messages that would be output to the console or during the Puppet run (this may be overridden by the `--logdest` command-line argument)
- The `last_run_summary.yaml` file contains a summary of the last run, with a count of the resources that were changed, the time taken to complete the run, and additional metrics

Beyond initial communication issues between the agents and the master, the bulk of Puppet troubleshooting revolves around failed catalog compilation and application.

With an idea of how the agent runs, we can now look closely at how one can configure Puppet as we examine the `puppet.conf` file in the next section.

Puppet configuration

Configuration of both the Puppet master and the agents (nodes) is done with the same configuration file, `puppet.conf`. This file is located in different directories, which depend on the version of Puppet that you are running—the open source version, or the commercial version, Puppet Enterprise. The different locations are summarized in the following table:

Operating system	Open source version	Puppet Enterprise
Linux/Mac OS X	`/etc/puppet/puppet.conf`	`/etc/puppetlabs/puppet/puppet.conf`
Windows*	`%PROGRAMDATA%\PuppetLabs\puppet\etc\puppet\puppet.conf`	

*Windows 2003 has a different location.

You may also override the name and location of this file with the config_file_name and config options respectively. The puppet.conf configuration file uses the INI-style syntax, which consists of multiple sections. The [main] section is used for settings that apply to both the master and the agent modes of Puppet. The [master] section is for the settings that only affect the master, while the [agent] section is used to specify settings that are specific to the agent.

Here is a sample puppet.conf file:

```
[main]
logdir = /var/log/puppet
rundir = /var/run/puppet
ssldir = $vardir/ssl

[agent]
classfile = $vardir/classes.txt
localconfig = $vardir/localconfig
```

There are many more configuration options available. Puppet provides a utility for viewing all the available configuration options. To view all the available configuration options, use puppet config print. To view the options for a specific section, add --section [section] to the command, as shown in the following example in the agent section:

```
t@mylaptop ~ $ puppet config print --section agent |sort |head -10
agent_catalog_run_lockfile = /home/thomas/.puppet/var/state/agent_
catalog_run.lock
agent_disabled_lockfile = /home/thomas/.puppet/var/state/agent_disabled.
lock
allow_duplicate_certs = false
allow_variables_with_dashes = false
always_cache_features = false
archive_file_server = puppet
archive_files = false
async_storeconfigs = false
autoflush = true
autosign = /home/thomas/.puppet/autosign.conf
```

The important configuration options on the agent (when trying to troubleshoot) are those that are associated with communication with the master. By default, a node will look for a master named `puppet`. This is actually specified by the `server` option in the agent section. You can verify this setting with the following command:

```
t@mylaptop ~ $ puppet config print server --section agent
puppet
```

Another important option is the port from which one should contact the master. By default, it is port 8140, but you can change this with the `masterport` option. It is also possible to specify another server for the certificate (SSL) signing. This is specified by using the `ca_server` option.

As mentioned previously, the node will use the `certname` option to specify its own name when communicating with the master. When troubleshooting, it can be useful to specify a different `certname` option for a node in order to force the generation of a new certificate. You may also find it useful to specify the `certname` option with an appended domain, which is generally known as the **fully qualified domain name (FQDN)** of the node.

In summary, when you are troubleshooting the communication between the nodes and the master, the following options are important in determining the servers that will be contacted and the names that will be used in the communication:

- `server`: This is the name of the master server
- `ca_server`: This is the name of the CA server
- `certname`: This is the name of the node that has to be used in the certificate
- `masterport`: This is port 8140 by default

If you are new to the Puppet environment that you are troubleshooting, it is also useful to know the values of the following options:

- `config_file_name`: This is `puppet.conf`; this is rarely overridden
- `confdir`: This is the directory containing the configuration files of Puppet
- `config`: This is a combination of `confdir/config_file_name`
- `vardir`: This is a directory that contains variable files, and it has a value of `/var/lib/puppet` by default
- `ssldir`: This is the directory that contains the SSL certificates, and it has a value of `$vardir/ssl` by default

puppet help

Most commands on Unix-like operating systems provide a manual or man page. The man page provides information on the available options and general guidance on using the command. Puppet initially chose not to follow this standard and instead used the help argument when calling the puppet command to specify documentation. Recent versions of Puppet have included manual pages for specific subcommands of the Puppet command-line tool. To access an individual manual page, type man puppet-[subcommand]. For example, to access the manual page on using puppet help, use man puppet-help. You can also access the same manual page using puppet man help.

The available help topics for a recent edition of Puppet are shown in the following screenshot:

```
t@mylaptop ~ $ puppet help

Usage: puppet <subcommand> [options] <action> [options]

Available subcommands:

    agent              The puppet agent daemon
    apply              Apply Puppet manifests locally
    ca                 Local Puppet Certificate Authority management.
    catalog            Compile, save, view, and convert catalogs.
    cert               Manage certificates and requests
    certificate        Provide access to the CA for certificate management.
    certificate_request  Manage certificate requests.
    certificate_revocation_list  Manage the list of revoked certificates.
    config             Interact with Puppet's settings.
    describe           Display help about resource types
    device             Manage remote network devices
    doc                Generate Puppet documentation and references
    facts              Retrieve and store facts.
    file               Retrieve and store files in a filebucket
    filebucket         Store and retrieve files in a filebucket
    help               Display Puppet help.
    inspect            Send an inspection report
    instrumentation_data  Manage instrumentation listener accumulated data. DEPRECATED.
    instrumentation_listener  Manage instrumentation listeners. DEPRECATED.
    instrumentation_probe  Manage instrumentation probes. Deprecated
    key                Create, save, and remove certificate keys.
    kick               Remotely control puppet agent
    man                Display Puppet manual pages.
    master             The puppet master daemon
    module             Creates, installs and searches for modules on the Puppet Forge.
    node               View and manage node definitions.
    parser             Interact directly with the parser.
    plugin             Interact with the Puppet plugin system.
    queue              Deprecated queuing daemon for asynchronous storeconfigs
    report             Create, display, and submit reports.
    resource           The resource abstraction layer shell
    resource_type      View classes, defined resource types, and nodes from all manifests.
    secret_agent       Mimics puppet agent.
    status             View puppet server status.

See 'puppet help <subcommand> <action>' for help on a specific subcommand action.
See 'puppet help <subcommand>' for help on a specific subcommand.
Puppet v3.7.4
t@mylaptop ~ $
```

For more information about a specific command, issue the command after `puppet help`. For example, for more information on `puppet config`, use `puppet help config`. This is demonstrated in the following code:

```
t@mylaptop ~ $ puppet help config


USAGE: puppet config<action> [--section SECTION_NAME]


This subcommand can inspect and modify settings from Puppet's

'puppet.conf' configuration file. For documentation about individual
settings,

see http://docs.puppetlabs.com/references/latest/configuration.html.


OPTIONS:
  --render-as FORMAT            - The rendering format to use.

  --verbose                     - Whether to log verbosely.

  --debug                       - Whether to log debug information.

  --section SECTION_NAME        - The section of the configuration file
to

interact with.


ACTIONS:
print     Examine Puppet's current settings.
setSet Puppet's settings.


See 'puppet man config' or 'man puppet-config' for full help.
```

You can also add subcommands to have even more specific information returned by the command, as follows:

```
t@mylaptop ~ $ puppet help config print


USAGE: puppet config print [--section SECTION_NAME] (all | <setting>
[<setting> ...]


Prints the value of a single setting or a list of settings.
```

```
OPTIONS:
  --render-as FORMAT            - The rendering format to use.
  --verbose                     - Whether to log verbosely.
  --debug                       - Whether to log debug information.
  --section SECTION_NAME        - The section of the configuration file
to
interact with.


See 'puppet man config' or 'man puppet-config' for full help.
```

The output of puppet help shows all the available arguments for the
Puppet command-line utility. We will now see the usefulness of a selection
of these arguments.

puppet resource

Using puppet resource can be a valuable troubleshooting tool. When you are
diagnosing a problem, puppet resource can be used to inspect a node and verify
how Puppet sees the state of a resource. For example, if we had a Linux node
running an SSH daemon (sshd), we could ask Puppet about the state of the sshd
service using puppet resource, as follows:

```
t@mylaptop ~ $ sudo puppet resource service sshd
service { 'sshd':
ensure => 'running',
enable => 'true',
}
```

As you can see, Puppet returned the current status of the service in Puppet code.
By using puppet resource, we can query the node for any resource type that is
known to Puppet. For instance, we can do this to view the status of the bind package
of a node, as follows:

```
t@mylaptop ~ $ sudo puppet resource package bind
package { 'bind':
ensure => 'absent',
}
```

We can also inspect the settings for a file, as follows:

```
t@mylaptop ~ $ sudo puppet resource file /etc/resolv.conf
file { '/etc/resolv.conf':
ensure   => 'file',
content  => '{md5}463bd26e077bc01a9368378737ef5bf0',
ctime    => '2015-03-02 21:04:21 -0800',
group    => '0',
mode     => '644',
mtime    => '2015-03-02 21:04:21 -0800',
owner    => '0',
selrange => 's0',
selrole  => 'object_r',
seltype  => 'net_conf_t',
seluser  => 'system_u',
type     => 'file',
}
```

puppet apply

When troubleshooting, it can often be useful to apply a small chunk of code rather than a whole catalog. By using `puppet apply`, you can specify a manifest file, which can be applied directly to a node. For example, to create a file named `/tmp/trouble` on the local node with the content `Hello, Troubleshooter!`, create the following manifest file named `trouble.pp`:

```
file {'/tmp/trouble':
  content => "Hello, Troubleshooter!\n"
}
```

When we run `puppet apply` on this manifest, Puppet will create the `/tmp/trouble` file as expected:

```
t@mylaptop ~ $ puppet apply trouble.pp
Notice: Compiled catalog for mylaptop in environment production in 0.21
seconds
Notice: /Stage[main]/Main/File[/tmp/trouble]/ensure: defined content as
'{md5}7b6223913adac8607e89a7c2f11744d0'
Notice: Finished catalog run in 0.03 seconds
t@mylaptop ~ $ cat /tmp/trouble
Hello, Troubleshooter!
```

When troubleshooting, it can be useful to add the `--debug` option when running `puppet apply`. Puppet will print information about how facts were compiled for the node, in addition to debugging information related to the application of resources.

puppet parser validate

The command-line utility can also be used to verify the syntax of your manifests. This can be useful when trying to find an issue with the compilation of your catalog. You can verify individual files by adding them as arguments to the command. For instance, the following manifest has a syntax error:

```
file {'bad':
ensure => 'directory',
path    => '/tmp/bad'
owner   => 'root',
}
```

We can verify this with `puppet parser validate`, which shows the following error:

```
t@mylaptop ~/trouble/01 $ puppet parser validate bad.pp
Error: Could not parse for environment production: Syntax error at
'owner'; expected '}' at /home/thomas/trouble/01/bad.pp:4
```

As you can see, there should be a comma after `'/tmp/bad'` since there is another attribute specified for the file resource.

I find myself using this command often enough to use the `ppv` alias for `puppet parser validate`.

Log files and the catalog

Logging in Puppet can be enabled on a client node (agent) with the `--debug` option to Puppet agent. This will output a lot of information. Each plugin file will be displayed as it is being read and executed. Once the catalog compiles, as each resource is applied to the machine, debugging information will be shown on the agent.

However, when you are debugging, your catalog may fail to compile. If this is the case, then you will need to examine the logs on the master. Where the logs are kept on the master depends on the way you have your master configured. The Puppet master process can be run either through a Ruby HTTP library named WEBrick, or via Passenger on a web server such as Apache or Nginx. Also, a third option now exists. You can also use the `puppetserver` application, which is a combination of JRuby and Clojure.

puppet master

Both the WEBrick and Passenger methods of running a Puppet master are equivalent to running `puppet master` from the command line. The configuration options for the Puppet master can be viewed with `puppet help master`.

By default, Puppet will log using `syslog` to the system logs (usually `/var/log/messages`). You can change this by making the `--logdest` option point at a file (`logdest` is used to specify the destination for log files, `logdest` may one of `syslog`, `console`, or the path to a file). If you are running the WEBrick server, then you can start the server like this:

```
# puppet master --logdest /var/log/puppet/master.log
```

> When using Passenger, you will have a `config.ru` file, which is installed with the `puppet-passenger` package. You can add the additional logging options to this file.

To enable the debugging of logs, add the `--debug` option in addition to the `--logdest` option. You may also enable the `--verbose` option.

puppetserver

`puppetserver` is the new server for Puppet that is based on the server for PuppetDB. It uses a **Java Virtual Machine (JVM)** to run JRuby for the Puppet Server. This mechanism also uses Clojure. Puppet Labs has already made `puppetserver` the default Puppet master implementation for the new installations of Puppet Enterprise. The configuration of `puppetserver` is different from the Puppet master configuration. The server is configured by files that are located in `/etc/puppetserver` by default. Since the server is running through a JVM, it uses the Logback library. The configuration for Logback is in `/etc/puppetserver/logback.xml`. To enable debug logs, edit this file and change the log level from `info` to `debug`, as follows:

```
<root level="debug">
<!--<appender-ref ref="STDOUT"/>-->
<appender-ref ref="${logappender:-DUMMY}" />
<appender-ref ref="F1"/>
</root>
```

Changes made to this file are recognized immediately by the server. There is no need to restart the service. For entirely too much information, try setting the level to `trace`. More information on `puppetserver` can be found at `https://github.com/puppetlabs/puppet-server`.

jq

When the catalog is compiled for a node, the master will send the catalog to the node. The node will store the catalog in the client_data subdirectory of /var/lib/puppet. The catalog will be in the JSON format (previous versions of Puppet used the YAML format for catalogs). Reading the JSON files is not as simple as reading the YAML files. A tool that can help make things easier is jq, a command-line JSON processor. You can use it to search through the JSON files. For instance, to view the classes within a catalog, use the following:

```
$ jq '.data.classes[]' <hostname.json
"settings"
"default"
```

To view the resources defined in the catalog, use the following command:

```
$ jq '.data.resources[]'<hostname.json
```

To filter out the resources tagged with a specific tag, use "class" as follows:

```
jq '.data.resources[] | select(.tags[] == "class")' <hostname.json
```

Once you learn the syntax for jq, searching through large catalogs becomes an easy task. This can help you find out where your resources are defined quickly. More information on jq can be found at http://stedolan.github.io/jq/.

Communication issues

Before you can begin debugging complex catalog problems, you need your nodes to communicate with each other. Communication problems between nodes and the master can either be network-related or certificate-related (SSL).

Network-related problems

When the Puppet agent is started on a node, one of the first things that the agent does is look up the value for the server option. You can either specify this with --server on the command line, or with server=[hostname] in the puppet.conf configuration file. By default, Puppet will look for a server named puppet. If it cannot find one named puppet, it will then try puppet.[your domain].

 What Puppet believes to be your domain may be obtained by running facter domain.

When you are debugging the initial communication problems, you need to first verify that your nodes can find the Puppet master. For Unix systems, the way in which the system searches for a machine by name is called the `gethostbyname` system call. This system call uses the **Name Service Switch** (**NSS**) library to find a host in a number of databases. NSS is configured by the `/etc/nsswitch.conf` file. The line in this file that is used to find hosts by their respective names is the hosts line. The default configuration on most of the systems is the following:

```
hosts:   files dns
```

This line means that the system will search for hosts by name in the local files first. Then, if the host is not found, it will search in the Internet **Domain Name System** (**DNS**). The local file that is first consulted is `/etc/hosts`. This file contains static host entries. If you inherited your Puppet environment, you should look in this file for statically defined Puppet entries. If the machine `puppet` or `puppet.[domain]` is not found in `/etc/hosts`, the system then queries the DNS to find the host. The DNS is configured with the `/etc/resolv.conf` file on the Unix systems.

> When troubleshooting, be aware that the `domain` fact is calculated using a combination of calls to the utility hostname and looking for a `domain` line in `/etc/resolv.conf`.

This file is known as the resolver configuration file. It's important to verify that you can reach the servers listed in the `nameserver` lines in this file. Your file may contain a search line. This line lists the domains that will be appended to your search queries. Consider a situation where the search line is as follows:

```
search example.com external.example.com internal.example.com
```

When you search for Puppet, the system will first search for `puppet`, then `puppet.example.com`, then `puppet.external.example.com`, and finally `puppet.internal.example.com`.

Several utilities exist for the testing of DNS. Among these utilities, `host` and `dig` are the most common. An older utility, `nslookup`, may also be used. To lookup the `ipaddress` option of the default Puppet Server, use the following:

```
t@mylaptop ~ $ host puppet
Host puppet not found: 3(NXDOMAIN)
```

In this example, the host `puppet` is not found. Yet, I know that this node works as expected. Remember that the system uses the `gethostbyname` system call when looking up the Puppet Server. Another utility on the system uses this call—the `ping` utility. When we try to ping the Puppet Server, this succeeds, and the output is as follows:

```
t@mylaptop ~ $ ping -c 1 puppet
PING localhost (127.0.0.1) 56(84) bytes of data.
64 bytes from localhost (127.0.0.1): icmp_seq=1 ttl=64 time=0.093 ms
--- localhost ping statistics ---
1 packets transmitted, 1 received, 0% packet loss, time 0ms
rtt min/avg/max/mdev = 0.093/0.093/0.093/0.000 ms
```

As you can see, the loopback address (`127.0.0.1`) is being used for the Puppet Server. We can verify that this information is coming from the `/etc/hosts` file using `grep`:

```
t@mylaptop ~ $ grep puppet /etc/hosts
127.0.0.1         localhostlocalhost.localdomainmylaptop localhost4
localhost4.localdomain4 mylaptop.example.com puppet.example.com puppet
```

Remembering the difference between using `host` or `dig` and using the `gethostbyname` system call can quickly help you find problems with your configuration. Adding an entry to `/etc/hosts` for your Puppet Server also bypasses any DNS problems that you may have in the initial configuration of your nodes.

Netcat

The next step in diagnosing network issues is verifying that you can reach the Puppet Server on the `masterport`, which is by default TCP port 8140. The `masterport` number may be changed, though. So, you should first confirm the port number using `puppet config print masterport`. One of the simplest tests to verify that you can reach the Puppet Server on port 8140 is to use **Netcat**. Netcat is known as the Swiss Army knife of network tools. You can do many interesting things with Netcat. More information about Netcat is available at `http://nmap.org/ncat/`.

There are several versions of Netcat available. The version installed on the most recent distributions is Ncat. The rewrite was done by Nmap (for more information, visit `https://nmap.org`).

To verify that you can reach port 8140 on your Puppet Server, issue the following command:

```
# nc -v puppet 8140
Connection to puppet 8140 port [tcp/*] succeeded!
```

If your Puppet Server was inaccessible, you will see an error message that looks like this:

```
nc: connect to puppet port 8140 (tcp) failed: Connection refused
```

If you see a Connection refused error as in the preceding output, this may indicate that there is a host-based firewall on the Puppet Server that is refusing the connection. Connection refusal means that you were able to contact the server, but the server did not permit the communication on the specified port. The first step in troubleshooting this type of problem is to verify that the Puppet Server is listening for connections on the port. The lsof utility can do this for you, as shown in the following code:

```
[root@puppet ~]# lsof -i :8140
COMMAND  PID    USER    FD    TYPE DEVICE SIZE/OFF NODE NAME
java    1960 puppet    18r   IPv6 22323      0t0   TCP *:8140 (LISTEN)
```

My Puppet Server is running the java process because puppetserver runs inside a JVM. We see java as the process name in the lsof output. If you do not see any output here, then you will know that your Puppet Server is not listening on the 8140 port.

If you do see a line with the LISTEN text, then your Puppet Server is listening and a firewall is blocking the communication. Host-based firewalls on Linux are configured with the firewalld system or iptables, depending on your distribution. More information on these two systems can be found at http://en.wikipedia.org/wiki/Iptables and https://fedoraproject.org/wiki/FirewallD.

> Ubuntu distributions also include an Uncomplicated Firewall (ufw) utility to configure iptables. BSD-based systems will use the Berkeley Packet Filter (pf) or IPFilter. Knowing how to configure your host-based firewall configuration is a key troubleshooting skill.

If you are familiar with firewall configuration, you can add port 8140 to the allow list and solve the problem. If you are new to firewall configuration, you may choose to temporarily disable the firewall to aid your troubleshooting. Although a perimeter firewall is often a better solution, host-based firewalls should be used wherever possible to avoid accidentally or unintentionally exposing ports on your servers. When you have fixed the problem, turn the host-based firewall back on. On an Enterprise Linux-based distribution, the following will disable the host-based firewall:

```
[root@puppet state]# service iptables stop
iptables: Setting chains to policy ACCEPT: filter        [  OK  ]
iptables: Flushing firewall rules:                       [  OK  ]
iptables: Unloading modules:                             [  OK  ]
```

If removing your host-based firewall does not solve your communication issue and you have verified that the service is listening on the correct port, then you will have to resort to advanced network troubleshooting tools.

Tools that may help in this case are `mtr` and `traceroute`. It is important to note that, even if a ping test fails, you may still be able to reach your Puppet Server on the `masterport`. The ping utility uses ICMP packets, which may be blocked or restricted on your network. If the `netcat` test still fails after addressing the firewall concerns, then you should try the `mtr` utility to check whether you can find where your communication is not reaching the server. For example, to test connectivity with the `puppet` server, issue the following command:

```
# mtr puppet
```

As an example, from my laptop, the following is the `mtr` output when attempting to reach `https://puppetlabs.com/`:

```
                           My traceroute  [v0.85]
mylaptop (0.0.0.0)                                        Wed Mar  4 21:57:14 2015
Keys:  Help   Display mode   Restart statistics   Order of fields   quit
                                              Packets               Pings
 Host                                        Loss%   Snt   Last   Avg  Best  Wrst StDev
 1. DD-WRT                                    0.0%   112   23.1   4.8   1.5  23.1   3.9
 2. ???
 3. te-0-1-0-22-sur03.bellevue.wa.seattle.comcast.net  0.9%   112   21.8  16.4  11.2  42.7   5.6
 4. be-40-ar01.seattle.wa.seattle.comcast.net  0.0%   111   14.6  17.5  12.5  32.1   4.1
 5. he-1-3-0-0-10-cr01.seattle.wa.ibone.comcast.net  0.0%   111   13.2  20.1  13.0 108.6   9.6
 6. he-2-13-0-0-cr01.miami.fl.ibone.comcast.net  0.0%   111   30.2  18.9  13.0  36.6   5.5
 7. as36351-1-c.seattle.wa.ibone.comcast.net   0.0%   111   13.8  19.3  12.8  47.1   7.1
 8. ae0.bbr01.cs01.den01.networklayer.com      0.0%   111   45.6  46.6  39.2  91.4   7.7
 9. ae12.bbr02.eq01.dal03.networklayer.com     1.8%   111   65.1  67.1  60.8 150.3   9.5
10. po32.dsr02.dllstx3.networklayer.com        0.0%   111  111.3  67.9  60.8 111.3   7.7
11. po31.dsr01.dllstx2.networklayer.com        0.0%   111   66.2  68.1  60.7 186.4  12.8
```

If you were unable to reach the Puppet Server, the last line in the host list would be ???. The line immediately preceding the ??? line would be the point at which the line of communication between the node and master was broken.

After you have verified that the network communication between the node and master is working as expected, the next issue that you should resolve is certificates.

SSL-related problems

Puppet uses X509 certificates to secure the communication between nodes and the master. As a Puppet administrator, you should know how the SSL certificates and a CA works.

Your infrastructure may have a separate server that acts as a CA for your Puppet installation. The CA is the certificate that is used to sign all the certificates that are generated by your master(s). If your CA is a separate server, the ca_server option will be specified in the puppet.conf file.

Although the server may be specified from the command line when running puppet agent, the ca_server option cannot.

By default, the CA certificate is generated on the first run of either the Puppet master or puppetserver. The certificate is stored in /var/lib/puppet/ssl/ca/ca_crt. pem for the **Open Source Puppet (OSS)** or /etc/puppetlabs/puppet/ssl/ca/ca_ crt.pem for **Puppet Enterprise (PE)**. To view the information in the certificate, use OpenSSL's x509 utility, as follows:

```
# openssl x509 -in ca_crt.pem -text
Certificate:
    Data:
        Version: 3 (0x2)
        Serial Number: 1 (0x1)
    Signature Algorithm: sha256WithRSAEncryption
        Issuer: CN=Puppet CA: puppet.example.com
        Validity
            Not Before: Feb 28 06:29:29 2015 GMT
            Not After : Feb 28 06:29:29 2020 GMT
        Subject: CN=Puppet CA: puppet.example.com
        Subject Public Key Info:
```

```
Public Key Algorithm: rsaEncryption
    Public-Key: (4096 bit)
    Modulus:
        00:99:2f:50:c4:5a:9c:e9:3a:4a:f0:1b:9b:9e:d1:
```
. . .

If you are new to the openssl command-line utility, try running openssl help (help is not actually an option, but it will cause the openssl command to print helpful information). Each of the subcommands to the openssl utility has its own Unix manual page. The manual page for the x509 subcommand can be found using man x509.

The preceding information shows that the CA certificate was automatically generated and has a five-year expiry. 5 years has been the default expiry time for some time now, and many Puppet installations are nearly 5 years old and require the generation of new CA certificates. If everything suddenly stopped working, you may wish to verify the expiry date of your CA. In addition to the expiry time, we can see the subject of the certificate, puppet.example.com. This is the name that Puppet has given to the CA based on the hostname and domain facts when the master/Puppet Server was started.

If you are diagnosing a certificate issue, you can first start by downloading the CA certificate. This can be done with the curl or wget utilities. In this example, we will use curl and pass the --insecure option to curl (since we have not downloaded the CA yet and cannot verify the certificate at this point), as follows:

```
$ curl --insecure https://puppet:8140/production/certificate/ca
-----BEGIN CERTIFICATE-----

MIIFfjCCA2agAwIBAgIBATANBgkqhkiG9w0BAQsFADAoMSYwJAYDVQQDDB1QdXBw

ZXQgQ0E6IHB1cHB1dC51eGFtcGxlLmNvbTAeFw0xNTAyMjgwNjI5MjlaFw0yMDAy
```
. . .

We can use a pipe (|) to direct the curl output to openssl and verify the certificate, as follows:

```
$ curl --insecure https://puppet:8140/production/certificate/ca |openssl
x509 -text
  % Total    % Received % Xferd  Average Speed   Time    TimeTime
Current
Dload  Upload   Total   Spent    Left  Speed
```

```
100  1964  100  1964    0     0   6684      0 --:--:-- --:--:-- --:--:-
-  6680
Certificate:
    Data:
        Version: 3 (0x2)
        Serial Number: 1 (0x1)
    Signature Algorithm: sha256WithRSAEncryption
        Issuer: CN=Puppet CA: puppet.example.com
        Validity
            Not Before: Feb 28 06:29:29 2015 GMT
            Not After : Feb 28 06:29:29 2020 GMT
        Subject: CN=Puppet CA: puppet.example.com
        Subject Public Key Info:
            Public Key Algorithm: rsaEncryption
                Public-Key: (4096 bit)
                Modulus:
                    00:99:2f:50:c4:5a:9c:e9:3a:4a:f0:1b:9b:9e:d1:
...
```

If the CA certificate verifies correctly, the next step is to attempt to retrieve the certificate for your node. You can do this by first downloading the CA certificate to a local file as follows:

```
$ curl --insecure https://puppet:8140/production/certificate/ca >ca_crt.
pem
  % Total    % Received % Xferd  Average Speed   Time     TimeTime
Current
Dload  Upload   Total   Spent    Left  Speed
100  1964  100  1964    0     0   6851      0 --:--:-- --:--:-- --:--:-
-  6867
```

In this example, my hostname is `mylaptop`. I will attempt to download my certificate from the master using `curl` (verifying the communication with the previously downloaded CA certificate):

```
$ curl --cacertca_crt.pem https://puppet:8140/production/certificate/
mylaptop
-----BEGIN CERTIFICATE-----
MIIFcTCCA1mgAwIBAgIBBDANBgkqhkiG9w0BAQsFADAoMSYwJAYDVQQDDB1QdXBw
ZXQgQ0E6IHB1cHB1dC51eGFtcGx1LmNvbTAeFw0xNTAzMDEwNjMzMDdaFw0yMDAy
...
```

As you can see, this succeeded. If we pipe the output to OpenSSL, we see that the subject of the certificate is `mylaptop` and the certificate has not expired:

```
$ curl --cacertca_crt.pem https://puppet:8140/production/certificate/
mylaptop |openssl x509 -text
  % Total    % Received % Xferd  Average Speed   Time     TimeTime
Current
Dload  Upload   Total   Spent    Left  Speed
100  1948  100  1948    0     0   6155      0 --:--:-- --:--:-- --:--:-
-  6145
Certificate:
    Data:
        Version: 3 (0x2)
        Serial Number: 4 (0x4)
    Signature Algorithm: sha256WithRSAEncryption
        Issuer: CN=Puppet CA: puppet.example.com
        Validity
            Not Before: Mar  1 06:33:07 2015 GMT
            Not After : Feb 29 06:33:07 2020 GMT
        Subject: CN=mylaptop
...
```

Since we previously downloaded the CA certificate, we can also verify this certificate by using the `verify` subcommand. To use `verify`, we will give the path to the CA certificate that was previously downloaded, and the client certificate that we just downloaded, as follows:

```
$ openssl verify -CAfile ca_crt.pem mylaptop.pem
mylaptop.pem: OK
```

If your master failed to return a certificate in the previous step, use `puppet cert` on the master to find the certificate. For the `mylaptop` example, issue the following commands:

```
[root@puppet ~]# puppet cert --list mylaptop
+ "mylaptop" (SHA256) 76:05:4E:C6:25:5F:04:63:A3:B7:5D:45:C9:60:48:DF:24:
0D:B7:3E:4D:9F:75:5E:C8:9F:64:1D:56:34:C2:D2
```

If the certificate is present but unsigned, the output will have a missing + symbol at the beginning, like this:

```
[root@puppet ~]# puppet cert --list mylaptop
  "mylaptop" (SHA256) 87:B3:28:31:B6:A4:3D:4A:BE:E0:4B:BD:DE:24:28:74:E1:
00:8A:09:91:3C:CD:B5:17:92:73:44:A1:41:C9:9E
```

If the certificate is not present, the output will look like this:

```
Error: Could not find a certificate for mylaptop
```

A common problem with certificates is an old certificate or a mismatch between the `ca_server`/`master` and the `node`. The simplest solution to this sort of problem is to remove the certificate from both machines and start again.

To remove the certificate on the `ca_server`, use `puppet cert clean` with the appropriate hostname, as follows:

```
[root@puppet ~]# puppet cert clean mylaptop
Notice: Revoked certificate with serial 6
Notice: Removing file Puppet::SSL::Certificate mylaptop at '/var/lib/
puppet/ssl/ca/signed/mylaptop.pem'
Notice: Removing file Puppet::SSL::Certificate mylaptop at '/var/lib/
puppet/ssl/certs/mylaptop.pem'
```

As mentioned in the output, the certificates are stored in the subdirectories of `/var/lib/puppet/ssl`. If the `puppet cert clean` command does not remove the certificate, you can remove the files manually from this location.

On the node, remove `private_key` and `certificate` from the `/var/lib/puppet/ssl` directory manually (there is no automatic way to do this). Alternatively, you can choose to remove the entire `/var/lib/puppet/ssl` directory and have the node download the CA certificate again.

This location is different for Puppet Enterprise. Puppet Enterprise stores certificates in `/etc/puppetlabs/puppet/ssl`. This often involves less work as compared to that of finding all the files that need to be removed.

When we ran `puppet cert clean` on the master, one of the output lines mentioned that the certificate has been revoked. X509 certificates can be revoked. The list of certificates that have been revoked is kept in the **Certificate Revocation List (CRL)**, which is in the `ca_crl.pem` file in `/var/lib/puppet/ssl/ca`.

We can use OpenSSL's `crl` utility to inspect the CRL, as follows:

```
[root@puppetca]# opensslcrl -in ca_crl.pem -text
Certificate Revocation List (CRL):
        Version 2 (0x1)
    Signature Algorithm: sha1WithRSAEncryption
        Issuer: /CN=Puppet CA: puppet.example.com
        Last Update: Mar  5 06:40:51 2015 GMT
        Next Update: Mar  3 06:40:52 2020 GMT
        CRL extensions:
            X509v3 Authority Key Identifier:
keyid:25:18:D4:0B:37:BD:BA:FE:70:D9:BB:17:8F:D9:84:EC:6D:30:76:71


            X509v3 CRL Number:
                2
Revoked Certificates:
    Serial Number: 06
        Revocation Date: Mar  5 06:40:52 2015 GMT
        CRL entry extensions:
            X509v3 CRL Reason Code:
                Key Compromise
```

As you can see, the certificate with the serial number 6 has been marked as revoked. The serial number is located within the certificate. When the master verifies a client, it will consult the CRL to verify that the serial number is not in the CRL.

More information on X509 certificates can be found at `https://www.ietf.org/rfc/rfc2459.txt` and `http://en.wikipedia.org/wiki/X.509`.

Summary

In this chapter, we introduced the main components of Puppet infrastructure. We highlighted the key points of a `puppet agent` run and the communication that takes place. We then moved on to talk about communication and how the X509 certificates are used by Puppet. We used Puppet's REST API to download and inspect certificates. In the next chapter, we will talk about Puppet manifests and how one can troubleshoot problems with code.

2
Writing Puppet Manifests

Puppet code is organized in manifests. In this chapter, we will cover how to write code in a way that reduces problems. We'll look at how one can configure editors to automatically correct code and keep it in style. Then, we'll look at how we can use tools to check the code for errors. Finally, we'll see how to use Git and Vagrant to automate the testing of our code.

Writing code

The Puppet style guide (for more information, visit `https://docs.puppetlabs.com/guides/style_guide.html`) was developed to define a common way of writing code that reduces errors. The style guide makes several suggestions to make your code more readable and consistent.

A common syntax error is to forget a comma between the attributes of a resource. Consider the following code:

```
file { '/tmp/oops':
mode    => '0644',
owner   => '0',
group   => '0'
content => 'Forgot something.'
}
```

In the preceding example, a comma is missing. Because of this, the catalog will fail to compile and show the following error:

```
Error: Could not parse for environment production: Syntax error at
'content'; expected '}' at oops.pp:5 on node trouble.example.com
```

This type of simple syntax error can be avoided by putting a comma at the end of every attribute, regardless of whether it is the final attribute or not. An advantage of this is that you can move attributes around within the definition and not worry about the presence or absence of commas.

When defining your resources, the style guide suggests that the `ensure` attribute should be the first attribute. This allows you to quickly tell whether the resource is being created or removed.

When you have a class that defines several resources and the ordering of the resources is complicated, chaining arrows can make this order more obvious. When using chaining arrows, the intent of the ordering will be much clearer when one defines the resources separately, away from the chaining arrows. For instance, if we have a relationship where a file resource requires another file resource and both of these files resources are required by an `exec` resource, this relationship can be shown as follows:

```
file {'/usr/share/myproject':
ensure => 'directory',
}->file {'/usr/share/myproject/myscript':
ensure=> 'file',
mode=> '0755',
content => "#!/bin/bash\necho My Script\n",
}->exec {'myscript':
command => '/usr/share/myproject/myscript',
path=> '/usr/bin:/bin'
}
```

For the preceding simple example, using the require metaparameters will be preferred. If we need to use chaining arrows, then putting them at the top of the manifest will make the preceding code much clearer, as shown in the following code:

```
File['myproject']->File['myscript']->Exec['myscript']

file {'myproject':
ensure => 'directory',
path    => '/usr/share/myproject',
}
file {'myscript':
ensure  => 'file',
path    => '/usr/share/myprojects/myscript',
mode    => '0755',
content => "#!/bin/bash\necho My Script\n",
}
```

```
exec {'myscript':
command => '/usr/share/myproject/myscript',
path    => '/usr/bin:/bin'
}
```

Using metaparameters is the preferred method of enforcing ordering on resources. In the preceding example, if we need to add another resource before the Exec['myscript'] resource, we have to remember to keep the ordering arrow statement updated. A situation where chaining arrows are particularly useful is when your resource requires several other resources and the require attribute is an array of resources. In this situation, the chaining arrows can make the require relationship more obvious.

Another recommendation of the style guide is that, when you need to indent code, you should use two spaces per block only. Do not use the literal tab character, as this may be displayed as a different length, depending on the editor in use. For similar reasons, use spaces when aligning arrows (=>). Using tabs will cause your text to render differently with different editors.

Your code should not contain any trailing whitespace. Trailing whitespaces and the two-space rules are important when using version control. Git will distinguish between two sections of identical code if one of them has trailing whitespace and/or uses tabs instead of spaces. Having commits that only differ in whitespace can obscure the real issues when you are trying to find the commit that caused a problem.

Use descriptive names for your classes. This can often be more important than you think. For example, if you have a class that configures the DNS resolver, then call it dns_resolver, resolv_conf, or something that points out that the module configures the DNS resolver. When in doubt, be more specific. If you use dns as the class name, it won't be immediately obvious that this class configures resolv.conf. It may seem that it is a class that configures **bind**, the **Internet Systems Consortium (ISC)** DNS server.

A module should configure only one thing on a system. Roles and profiles are used when you want to orchestrate modules to make them work together. For instance, many installations will include the configuration of the **Name Service Switch (NSS)** in their dns_resolver module. The NSS configuration file, nsswitch.conf, is used to configure the name service switcher, a system that is used to find hosts and for more than hostname resolution. The system can be configured to use DNS for hostname resolution, in addition to other protocols, including **Network Information Service (NIS)**, **Lightweight Directory Access Protocol (LDAP)**, and **System Security Services (SSS)**.

The `nsswitch.conf` file can also be used to configure the system to use one of the preceding systems (NIS, LDAP, and SSS) to look up **netgroups**. Netgroups are used by the **Network File System** (**NFS**) and older shell access protocols such as RSH to configure access to resources. The important thing to note here is that although it might seem appropriate to include the configuration of `nsswitch.conf` in the module that configures `resolv.conf`, the `nsswitch.conf` file is used by more than just the process of hostname resolution. Therefore, you should put the `nsswitch.conf` configuration in a module of its own.

Along similar lines, break up your module into subclasses wherever it seems appropriate. If your module has a configuration section that is easily separated from your installation process, then create two subclasses: `config` and `install`. This may prove very useful later when you are trying to debug a problem. You can include the subclasses one by one until you notice the aberrant behavior that you were trying to track down.

Editors

Syntax highlighting can be a huge help when you are writing code. If your editor colors your code the wrong color, you know visually that there is a syntax error. This can help you quickly find out where you forgot to close a quote. Configuring your editor to follow the style guidelines that were outlined in the previous section makes obeying the guidelines transparent. If you configure your editor to use two spaces instead of tabs, then you don't have to remember to check your code for tabs. In the next two sections, we will configure two of the most popular editors for Puppet code on Unix machines.

Vim

There are two modules that are used to configure `vim` to write Puppet code. One is the `puppetlabs` module, which is located at `https://github.com/puppetlabs/puppet/tree/master/ext/vim/`, and the other is the one developed by Tim Sharpe at `https://github.com/rodjek/vim-puppet`. On Linux systems, the Puppet packages from Puppet Labs install the VIM files in the system directories for you. You will need to choose one of the modules, as `vim` will only support one of them at a time.

 You may have to copy the files installed by the `puppetlabs` package into your own `~/.vim` directory to activate them.

To manually install the Puppet Labs `vim` module, from the preceding URL, download all the files into your `.vim` directory.

To use the module from Puppet Labs, add the following to your `.vimrc` file:

```
filetype plugin indent on
auBufRead,BufNewFile *.pp          set filetype=puppet
```

Your `.vimrc` file should also include options to use soft tabs (spaces) and set the number of spaces per tab to 2:

```
set tabstop=2
set shiftwidth=2
set expandtab
```

The `shiftwidth` option is useful if you want to indent blocks of code with Vim. This will force the indentation to consist of two spaces.

Both of these modules will automatically align your attribute arrows for resources.

> The Tim Sharpe module requires the Vim `tabular` module (for more information, visit `https://github.com/godlygeek/tabular`) to be installed for this feature to work.

Syntastic is another module that you may wish to consider. It checks the syntax automatically after saving files.

The advantage of Vim over other editors is that it is very lightweight. This means that starting up Vim is a quick operation. Vim is ideal for the developer who is editing many different files on many different machines. All Unix systems will have some variant of `vi` or `vim` installed for you to use. There are versions of Vim for Microsoft Windows and Mac OS X. Both of the preceding modules can be used with the Windows and Macintosh versions. The other main Unix editor is Emacs, which will be covered in the next section.

Emacs

Emacs is usually available on Unix systems, and versions are also available for Windows and Macintosh systems. Longtime users of Emacs will tell you that it is not an editor. Emacs is a highly extensible LISP system that features text editing. Like Vim, Emacs can also be optimized for Puppet development. As with Vim, when you install the packages from Puppet Labs, the `emacs` mode files are placed in the appropriate directories.

To manually install the Puppet-mode from Puppet Labs, download the files from the Puppet Labs GitHub repository by visiting `https://github.com/puppetlabs/puppet-syntax-emacs` and place them in your `.emacs.d` directory. The `puppet-mode-init.el` file is used to load the Puppet-mode automatically when you start Emacs. You'll need to copy this file and place it in either your `.emacs` file or your `.emacs.d/init.el` file.

Geppetto

Geppetto is an **integrated development environment (IDE)** developed by Puppet Labs to write Puppet code. It is based on the popular Java IDE, Eclipse. Geppetto is available at `http://puppetlabs.github.io/geppetto/index.html`. To install Geppetto, download the ZIP archive and then unzip the archive in your home directory. This will create a `geppetto` directory. To start Geppetto, run the Geppetto executable in the `geppetto` directory. When you first start Geppetto, it will be relatively blank, as shown in the following screenshot:

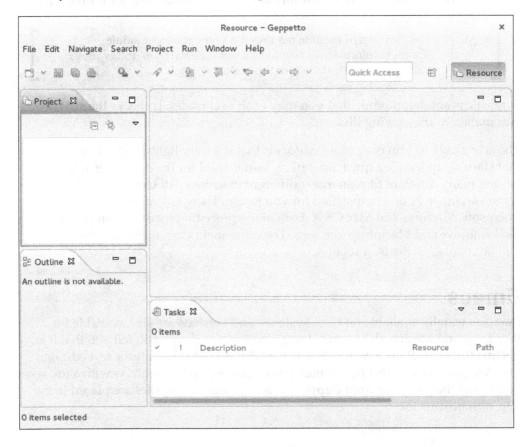

To work with your Puppet code in Geppetto, create a project. There are two templates for projects—Puppet project and Puppet module.

If you are working on your control repository, then use Puppet project. Otherwise, use the Puppet module setting.

If you already have your code in Git, you can import your existing project using the **Import** option from the **File** menu. Select **Projects from Git**, as shown in the following screenshot:

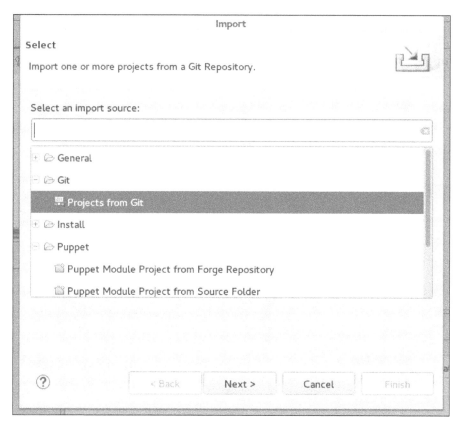

Next, locate your local repository and select it for import. When you are on the wizard selection screen, select **Import as general project**:

Once your project is imported, apply the Puppet nature to the project by selecting the **Add Puppet Nature** option, as follows:

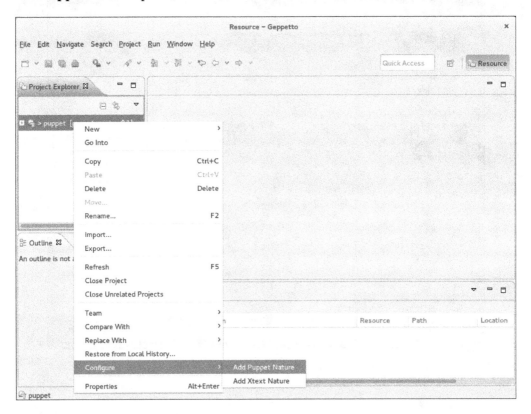

Then, you can double-click on the source files in your project and make changes to them.

Once you have finished making changes to your file(s), you can commit the changes back to your repository by right-clicking on your project and clicking on the **Team** option. In the submenu, select **Commit...**, as shown in the following screenshot:

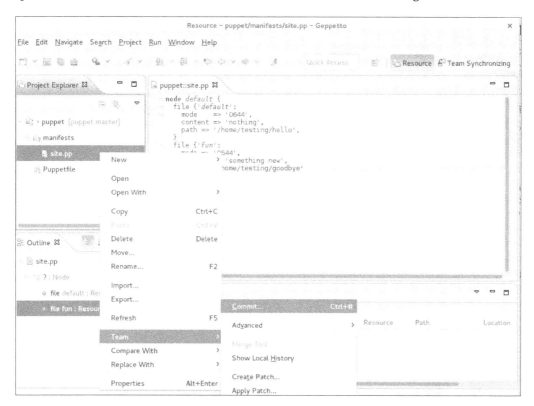

Most of the Git operations that you will need to perform can be found in the **Team** menu. You can rebase, merge, create branches, and update upstream repositories from within Geppetto. More information on Geppetto is available on the project site at `https://docs.puppetlabs.com/geppetto/4.0/`. A good resource is the PuppetConf video at `https://www.youtube.com/watch?v=TxeaEo2jKWQ`.

puppet-lint

Lint is the name given to a program that searches through code for non-ideal or nonportable syntax. The `puppet-lint` tool is a Lint tool for Puppet code. It will go through your Puppet code and point out the code that has the potential to be a problem. By default, `puppet-lint` uses the style-guide guidelines and will report problems such as lines that have more than 80 characters.

The puppet-lint tool is a Ruby gem and can be installed using the gem tool or as a package, depending on your distribution (for instance, Fedora calls this package rubygem-puppet-lint). To install it using Puppet, run the following puppet resource command:

```
$ sudo puppet resource package puppet-lint ensure=installed provider=gem
Notice: /Package[puppet-lint]/ensure: created
package { 'puppet-lint':
ensure => ['1.1.0'],
}
$ puppet-lint -v
puppet-lint 1.1.0
```

To test puppet-lint, add the following code to a manifest called lint.pp:

```
class linty {
file {"/tmp/lint":
mode        => 0644,
ensure      => 'false',
content => "$hostname.troubleshooting",
  }
}
```

Now run puppet-lint on the lint.pp manifest:

```
thomas@mylaptop:~/trouble/02                                    ×
t@mylaptop ~/trouble/02 $ puppet-lint lint.pp
ERROR: linty not in autoload module layout on line 1
WARNING: class not documented on line 1
WARNING: double quoted string containing no variables on line 2
WARNING: variable not enclosed in {} on line 5
WARNING: quoted boolean value found on line 4
WARNING: indentation of => is not properly aligned on line 3
WARNING: indentation of => is not properly aligned on line 4
WARNING: indentation of => is not properly aligned on line 5
WARNING: ensure found on line but it's not the first attribute on line 4
WARNING: unquoted file mode on line 3
t@mylaptop ~/trouble/02 $
```

As you can see, there are quite a few problems with our code. The line beginning with ERROR: is the most problematic. We called our manifest lint.pp, but the class is linty. To ensure that the autoloader is able to find the classes properly, you need to name your files the same as your classes. The solution is to change the name of the class to lint or change the name of the file to linty.pp.

Puppet will search through your Puppet code for appropriate files to load based on the "autoloader". All this means is that classes must be stored in files whose filenames match the class names.

The second line is a warning about documentation. We should document what our code is expected to do. The next line is a warning about style. The style guide suggests that you only use double quotes (") when quoting literal values (\n or ') or when you are including variables. Variables are only resolved when they are enclosed in double quotes.

The `puppet-lint` tool next complains that a variable isn't properly enclosed in braces ({ }). This is a style item, but enclosing variables in braces does make it easier to visually decide where a variable definition ends.

Variables within quotes should be enclosed in braces. Variables used as values to attributes should not. For example, the following is a syntax error:

```
file { 'test':
  content => ${variable}
}
```

The brace wrapping is only valid within quotes.

The next error reported is a failure to quote a Boolean value:

`WARNING: quoted boolean value found on line 4`

Boolean values should not be quoted. This can be a big problem in Puppet. Strings quoted as `"false"` or `'false'` both evaluate to *True* in Puppet. The only two things that evaluate to *False* in Puppet are the literal, unquoted `false` and the empty string, `""`. Never quote Booleans. In Puppet 4, this behavior changes, the empty string evaluates to *True*. This behavior is also observed when using the future parser option on Puppet versions 3.7 and above.

The next three lines complain about the alignment of the assignment arrows for attributes. This is really a style item. It makes your code "prettier" to have the arrows aligned.

`WARNING: ensure found on line but it's not the first attribute on line 4`

The preceding warning indicates that we have an `ensure` attribute, which is not the first attribute. This is an important warning from the standpoint of troubleshooting. If we have a resource with many attributes defined and the `ensure` attribute near the bottom of the list, we may miss the `ensure` attribute. We may waste time trying to troubleshoot why the resource isn't being created, only to find that the `ensure` attribute has been set to `false`.

Our next error is forgetting to quote the `mode` attribute of a file resource:

```
WARNING: unquoted file mode on line 3
```

Unless you are using a reserved word in the value, your value should be quoted. The mode of our file resource doesn't qualify as a reserved word. The most commonly used reserved words are `true`, `false`, `running`, `stopped`, and `manual`.

Fixing up our previous code, we have the following manifest (which is stored in `linty/manifests/init.pp`):

```
# class to test puppet-lint
class linty {
file {'/tmp/lint':
ensure  => false,
mode    => '0644',
content => "${::hostname}.troubleshooting",
  }
}
```

Now, when we run `puppet-lint` on our improved manifest, we get the output as shown in the following screenshot:

More information on `puppet-lint` can be found on the project's home page, `http://puppet-lint.com/`.

Testing code

When writing code, mistakes are bound to happen. There are several layers to troubleshooting the problems that will occur. In the next three sections, we'll look at some solutions to problems with your code, starting with the simplest layer to fix—the syntax.

Validating code

The `puppet-lint` tool is good at finding problems with style and certain syntax issues. For real syntax problems, Puppet has a built-in validation mode, `puppet parser validate`. To validate your code, run `puppet parser validate` against your manifest.

For example, the following manifest (`validate.pp`) has a syntax error that is easy to make:

```
 1 class validate
 2 (
 3   $who = "Me",
 4   $where = "Here",
 5 ) {
 6   file { 'why':
 7     path     => '/tmp/why'
 8     contents => "Por Que Dos?\n",
 9   }
10 }
11 include validate
```

When you run `puppet parser validate` against this manifest, you will see the following output:

```
thomas@mylaptop: ~/trouble/02                                          x
t@mylaptop ~/trouble/02 $ puppet parser validate validate.pp
Error: Could not parse for environment production: Syntax error at 'conten
ts'; expected '}' at /home/thomas/trouble/02/validate.pp:8
t@mylaptop ~/trouble/02 $
```

From the preceding output, we know that we should look at line 8 of the `validate.pp` file.

> If you are using `vim` to edit your files, you can tell `vim` to open the file to line 8 by issuing the following command:
>
> `t@mylaptop ~/trouble/02 $ vim validate.pp +8`

The problem is not on line 8; it is actually on line 7, where we've forgotten to add a comma at the end of the line. Add a comma now to the end of line 7 and run `puppet parser validate` again:

```
t@mylaptop ~/trouble/02 $ puppet parser validate validate.pp
t@mylaptop ~/trouble/02 $ echo $?
0
```

As you can see, by echoing the contents of $? (the return code variable for Bash), the return code of `puppet parser validate` is now 0. This indicates that the code has passed the syntax check. However, there is still a problem with the code. We passed the contents attribute to the `why` file resource. The correct attribute is `content`, not `contents`. The `puppet parser validate` command cannot check for this type of error. When we run `puppet apply` against our manifest, we see that Puppet cannot apply `validate.pp`:

```
t@mylaptop ~/trouble/02 $ puppet apply validate.pp
Error: Invalid parameter contents on File[why] at /home/thomas/
trouble/02/validate-comma.pp:9 on node mylaptop
Wrapped exception:
Invalid parameter contents
Error: Invalid parameter contents on File[why] at /home/thomas/
trouble/02/validate-comma.pp:9 on node mylaptop
```

We can fix this by changing `contents` to `content`. After making this change, we see that Puppet can apply the manifest properly:

```
t@mylaptop ~/trouble/02 $ puppet apply validate-content.pp
Notice: Compiled catalog for mylaptop in environment production in 0.29
seconds
Notice: /Stage[main]/Validate/File[why]/ensure: defined content as '{md5}
fd2d0b7e3484dc438e92df150e7192ca'
Notice: Finished catalog run in 0.06 seconds
```

> In previous versions of Puppet, this code would still have one more syntax error. The arguments to the class on lines 2 through 5 are incorrect. There is an extra comma on line 4. If these lines were combined into a single line, the extra comma would be more obvious:
>
> ```
> ( $who = "Me", $where = "Here",) {
> ```
>
> If you are writing code for the older versions of Puppet, be aware that this would cause Puppet to show an error and not compile the manifest. Newer versions of Puppet permit this syntax.

In the previous example, we saw that even `puppet parser validate` cannot save us from every error. Sometimes, it is better to try applying your code to a node when you are debugging. In the next section, we'll talk about a tool that makes live testing of your code easier.

Vagrant

When testing your Puppet code, it is useful to create test environments to apply your code live without affecting your production environments. Testing your code locally with virtual machines goes a long way in ensuring that your code will work in production.

Vagrant is a scripting tool for virtual machines. With Vagrant, you can automate the creation, configuration, and destruction of virtual machines on your local machine. The default virtual machine environment that is supported by Vagrant is VirtualBox. There are plugins to make KVM work with Vagrant as well as a supported plugin to work with VMware Fusion. The original reason behind choosing VirtualBox as the virtual machine platform is that VirtualBoxes has built-in client file redirection. This feature allows you to expose a directory on your host machine to your client VMs. As you will see, this can be very useful when you are debugging code.

Creating virtual boxes from scratch takes a long time. Vagrant reduces the time that is taken to deploy virtual machines by using base machines, which are termed **boxes** by Vagrant. A box is a base image that includes a Vagrant user and is configured to allow access to this user from the `vagrant` command. The Vagrant user also has the `sudo` rights on the box. When you want to deploy a virtual machine with Vagrant, Vagrant will clone the box image to a new virtual machine.

Vagrant is configured with a Ruby script file. The file is named `Vagrantfile`. You can create a new `Vagrantfile` in a directory by running `vagrant init`, as follows:

```
t@mylaptop ~/trouble/02 $ vagrant init
A 'Vagrantfile' has been placed in this directory. You are now
ready to 'vagrant up' your first virtual environment! Please read
the comments in the Vagrantfile as well as documentation on
'vagrantup.com' for more information on using Vagrant.
```

This will create a `Vagrantfile` with a base machine defined. To get started, download a base image from `puppetlabs`, as follows:

```
t@mylaptop ~/trouble/02 $ vagrant box add puppetlabs/ubuntu-14.04-64-puppet
==>box: Loading metadata for box 'puppetlabs/ubuntu-14.04-64-puppet'
box: URL: https://atlas.hashicorp.com/puppetlabs/ubuntu-14.04-64-puppet
This box can work with multiple providers! The providers that it
```

```
can work with are listed below. Please review the list and choose
the provider you will be working with.


1) virtualbox

2) vmware_desktop

3) vmware_fusion


Enter your choice: 1

==>box: Adding box 'puppetlabs/ubuntu-14.04-64-puppet' (v1.0.1) for
provider: virtualbox

box: Downloading: https://atlas.hashicorp.com/puppetlabs/boxes/ubuntu-
14.04-64-puppet/versions/1.0.1/providers/virtualbox.box

==>box: Successfully added box 'puppetlabs/ubuntu-14.04-64-puppet'
(v1.0.1) for 'virtualbox'!
```

We can now list the available boxes on our system to see the new box, as follows:

```
t@mylaptop ~/trouble/02 $ vagrant box list

puppetlabs/ubuntu-14.04-64-puppet (virtualbox, 1.0.1)
```

Now, we can update the `Vagrantfile` to use the new box, as follows:

```
Vagrant.configure(2) do |config|
config.vm.define "puppetmaster", primary: true do |puppet|
puppet.vm.box = "puppetlabs/ubuntu-14.04-64-puppet"
puppet.vm.hostname = "puppetmaster.example.com"
puppet.vm.network :forwarded_port, guest: 8140, host: 8140, id:
"puppet"
end
end
```

In the preceding configuration, we also added port 8140 (the Puppet port) to the Vagrant machine to allow the local machine to access the Puppet port on the virtual machine.

To start up `puppetmaster`, run `vagrant up`, as follows:

```
t@mylaptop ~/trouble/02 $ vagrant up

Bringing machine 'puppetmaster' up with 'virtualbox' provider...

==>puppetmaster: Importing base box 'puppetlabs/ubuntu-14.04-64-
puppet'...
```

```
==>puppetmaster: Matching MAC address for NAT networking...

==>puppetmaster: Checking if box 'puppetlabs/ubuntu-14.04-64-puppet' is
up to date...

==>puppetmaster: Setting the name of the VM: 02_
puppetmaster_1426745567888_13079

==>puppetmaster: Clearing any previously set network interfaces...

==>puppetmaster: Preparing network interfaces based on configuration...

puppetmaster: Adapter 1: nat

==>puppetmaster: Forwarding ports...

puppetmaster: 8140 => 8140 (adapter 1)

puppetmaster: 22 => 2222 (adapter 1)

==>puppetmaster: Booting VM...

==>puppetmaster: Waiting for machine to boot. This may take a few
minutes...

puppetmaster: SSH address: 127.0.0.1:2222

puppetmaster: SSH username: vagrant

puppetmaster: SSH auth method: private key

puppetmaster: Warning: Connection timeout. Retrying...

puppetmaster:

puppetmaster: Vagrant insecure key detected. Vagrant will automatically
replace

puppetmaster: this with a newly generated keypair for better security.

puppetmaster:

puppetmaster: Inserting generated public key within guest...

puppetmaster: Removing insecure key from the guest if its present...

puppetmaster: Key inserted! Disconnecting and reconnecting using new SSH
key...

==>puppetmaster: Machine booted and ready!

==>puppetmaster: Checking for guest additions in VM...

==>puppetmaster: Setting hostname...

==>puppetmaster: Mounting shared folders...

puppetmaster: /vagrant => /home/thomas/trouble/02
```

You can now SSH into the machine that you just created and verify the Puppet version on the machine using `vagrant ssh`:

```
t@mylaptop ~/trouble/02 $ vagrant ssh
Welcome to Ubuntu 14.04.2 LTS (GNU/Linux 3.16.0-30-generic x86_64)

 * Documentation:  https://help.ubuntu.com/
vagrant@puppetmaster:~$ puppet --version
3.7.4
```

For this simple example, start the Puppet master from the command line of your Vagrant machine, as follows:

```
root@puppetmaster:~# puppet master
```

Now, verify that the master is running using `lsof`:

```
root@puppetmaster:~# lsof -i :8140
COMMAND  PID   USER   FD    TYPE DEVICE SIZE/OFF NODE NAME
puppet   1765 puppet   7u   IPv4  13981      0t0  TCP *:8140 (LISTEN)
```

In another window on your host machine, configure the host machine to think that `puppetmaster.example.com` is located at `127.0.0.1`. On Unix systems, this will mean editing `/etc/hosts` and adding `puppetmaster.example.com` to the entry from `127.0.0.1`.

On my machine, this line looks like this:

```
127.0.0.1        localhostlocalhost.localdomainmylaptop puppetmaster.
example.com puppetmaster
```

With this change made, we can start puppet agent (I'll run the agent as myself instead of root here) and point the agent at your local machine (127.0.0.1):

```
t@mylaptop ~/trouble/02 $ puppet agent -t --server puppetmaster.example.
com
Info: Creating a new SSL key for mylaptop
Info: Caching certificate for ca
Info: csr_attributes file loading from /home/thomas/.puppet/csr_
attributes.yaml
Info: Creating a new SSL certificate request for mylaptop
```

```
Info: Certificate Request fingerprint (SHA256): D3:A8:C5:19:2E:A4:A9:7D:5
E:0F:4A:43:C7:81:72:F0:E2:43:A0:6B:EF:10:90:52:6A:04:FF:1D:31:23:B7:DB
```

```
Info: Caching certificate for ca
```

```
Exiting; no certificate found and waitforcert is disabled
```

The preceding console output shows that your host machine is communicating with puppetmaster. Now go back to the Vagrant machine and sign the certificate:

```
root@puppetmaster:~# puppet cert list
```

```
Warning: Setting templatedir is deprecated. See http://links.puppetlabs.
com/env-settings-deprecations
```

```
   (at /usr/lib/ruby/vendor_ruby/puppet/settings.rb:1139:in 'issue_
deprecation_warning')
```

```
   "mylaptop" (SHA256) D3:A8:C5:19:2E:A4:A9:7D:5E:0F:4A:43:C7:81:72:F0:E2:
43:A0:6B:EF:10:90:52:6A:04:FF:1D:31:23:B7:DB
```

```
root@puppetmaster:~# puppet cert sign mylaptop
```

```
Notice: Signed certificate request for mylaptop
```

```
Notice: Removing file Puppet::SSL::CertificateRequestmylaptop at '/var/
lib/puppet/ssl/ca/requests/mylaptop.pem'
```

Now when we run puppet agent again on our host machine, we see a clean Puppet run, as follows:

```
t@mylaptop ~/trouble/02 $ puppet agent -t --server puppetmaster.example.
com
```

```
Info: Caching certificate_revocation_list for ca
```

```
Info: Retrieving pluginfacts
```

```
Info: Retrieving plugin
```

```
Info: Caching catalog for mylaptop
```

```
Info: Applying configuration version '1426746780'
```

```
Notice: Finished catalog run in 0.04 seconds
```

Now that you have verified that the basic environment works as intended, we'll make this configuration more useful by taking advantage of the folder redirection that Vagrant provides. Back on the Puppet master, note that the directory that you created to keep your Vagrantfile is available to puppetmaster in the /vagrant location.

```
root@puppetmaster:~# cd /vagrant/
```

```
root@puppetmaster:/vagrant# cat Vagrantfile
```

```
# -*- mode: ruby -*-
# vi: set ft=ruby :

Vagrant.configure(2) do |config|
  config.vm.define "puppetmaster", primary: true do |puppet|
    puppet.vm.box = "puppetlabs/ubuntu-14.04-64-puppet"
    puppet.vm.hostname = "puppetmaster.example.com"
    puppet.vm.network :forwarded_port, guest: 8140, host: 8140, id: "puppet"
  end
end
```

As a simple example of how you can use Vagrant to speed up your development, create a simple site manifest in your working directory on your host machine, as follows:

```
node default {
  notify {"Default vagrant site.pp": }
}
```

Create a `manifests` directory and place the preceding code in `site.pp` in that directory.

Now back on your `puppetmaster` VM, edit `/etc/puppet/puppet.conf` and add a `manifestdir` option, which is a deprecated way of configuring Puppet. You should use `environment.conf`; we are using `manifestdir` here for illustration only:

```
manifestdir=/vagrant/manifests
```

Stop and restart the master on your `puppetmaster` using `pkill`, since we don't have a service configured:

```
root@puppetmaster:/vagrant# pkill puppet
root@puppetmaster:/vagrant# puppet master
```

Now, return to your host machine and run `puppet agent` again to see the notification that you created earlier, as follows:

```
t@mylaptop ~/trouble/02 $ puppet agent -t --server puppetmaster.example.com
Info: Retrieving pluginfacts
Info: Retrieving plugin
```

```
Info: Caching catalog for mylaptop
Info: Applying configuration version '1426747119'
Notice: Default vagrant site.pp
Notice: /Stage[main]/Main/Node[default]/Notify[Default vagrant site.pp]/
message: defined 'message' as 'Default vagrant site.pp'
Notice: Finished catalog run in 0.05 seconds
```

As you can see, the Puppet master used code from the home directory to compile the catalogs for nodes. This can make an extremely efficient testing mechanism for new code. In a full configuration, you would configure Puppet to look for the environments directory within a subdirectory of /vagrant. By using `environment.conf`, you can then include multiple module paths and replicate your production Puppet infrastructure on your personal machine. This can be a great way to troubleshoot problems locally without affecting your development environments.

More information on Vagrant can be found at `https://www.vagrantup.com/`, the project website.

Committing code

Version control is another big helper when you are troubleshooting a problem. Version control systems are great at keeping logs of changes and allowing you to revert changes when they introduce problems. Commit logs are only as good as you make them. When you make your commits, you should remember that the colleague who has to decipher the change you made won't know the reason behind your change. Your commit message should not include what has changed, but why it was changed or what you were attempting to do. If we are debugging a problem, there is a good chance that the change that was made didn't do what was intended.

Another reason to use version control is that version control systems can be configured to prevent the deployment of incorrect code. Git is the de facto standard version control mechanism for Puppet. In the next section, we'll see how we can configure Puppet to use the tools that we've previously discussed to check our code for errors before committing those changes.

Git hooks

Hooks are scripts run by Git. Git will run hook scripts based on the situation or the stage of deployment. There are several hooks that are run at different stages of the deployment of code. We are interested in the pre-commit hook—this hook is run before a commit is committed to the repository. There are several good examples for pre-commit hooks available. The Puppet Labs suggested hook runs `puppet parser validate` against all the files ending in the `.pp` extension. The script can be found at `http://projects.puppetlabs.com/projects/1/wiki/puppet_version_control`, the website of Puppet Labs. Copy the script from the page into the `.git/hooks` directory of your Git repository. The file should be named pre-commit and have the executable permissions set (755 usually).

To test the hook, try committing the following code with an obvious syntax error:

```
file {'something':
  path    => '/tmp/1',
  content => 'something'
  mode    => '0644',
}
```

When we add the file and then try to commit, we see the following output:

```
t@mylaptop ~/tmp/t $ git add init.pp
t@mylaptop ~/tmp/t $ git commit -m "adding init.pp"
Error: Could not parse for environment production: Syntax error at
'mode'; expected '}' at /home/thomas/tmp/t/init.pp:4
init.pp: Error: 1 syntax errors found, aborting commit.
```

The pre-commit script has prevented the commit from making it into the repository. Bu using pre-commit hooks, you can prevent the most common types of syntax error from entering your repository. The pre-commit hook is like a gatekeeper at the front door, stopping bad code from entering your environment and reducing the number of problems that you will need to troubleshoot. If you are concerned about adhering to the style guide, you can also have your pre-commit hook run `puppet-lint`. Many sites will use both checks (`puppet-lint` and `puppet parser validate`) to ensure that their code is free from error and style issues.

Using environments

Environments allow for the logical separation of different stages of development. A very common workflow for Puppet installations is to create multiple environments and promote code between the different environments. If you are fortunate enough to have Git in your installation, you can use Git branches as environments. This allows you to switch environments just by checking out a different branch. You can promote code between environments by merging branches. When creating your environments, production should be the endpoint in your code progression. A common starting point is dev, or development. Many installations will have a pre-development or a sandbox environment as well. When you have several environments, the progression between the environments should be well-defined and known to all of your Puppet developers.

Sandbox → Development → Quality Assurance → Performance Testing → Production

 Using the preceding names for environments will likely upset your developers, who don't enjoy typing so much. An actual implementation might use the following names:

sbx → dev → qa → perf → prod

Keeping these long-running branches allows you to follow the progression of your code through different environments. For the purpose of troubleshooting, environments allow you to isolate problems when they occur. A well-defined testing process between environments ensures that the code has been tested in several environments before it is promoted to your production equipment.

Personal branches

A great thing about Git branches is that they are nothing more than a reference to a point in your commit history. Branches are cheap and disposable. When a problem arises and you need to work on it without affecting other developers, you can create a bugfix branch to solve that issue. When you have finished fixing the problem, you can merge your branch back into the environment. Personal branches buy you a play space.

Summary

In this chapter, we looked at various ways to test our code for syntax and style issues. We configured editors to help us keep our code properly formatted. We then talked about Git and how we can configure it to automatically detect problems. We then talked about environments and how we can use them to test our code in staging environments before it is used in production. In the next chapter, we'll talk about the problems that are seen when organizing manifests into modules and how we can troubleshoot problems with templates.

3
Modules and Templates

As a Puppet developer or a system administrator, modules are how you deliver your code to the nodes. Modules are great for organizing your code into manageable chunks, but modules are also where you'll see most of your problems when troubleshooting. In this chapter, we will look at how the various parts of a module may cause issues. Most modules contain classes in a manifests directory, but modules can also include custom facts, functions, types, providers, as well as files and templates. Each of these components can be a source of error. We will address each of these components in the following sections, starting with classes.

In Puppet, the namespace of classes is referred to as the scope. Classes can have multiple nested levels of subclasses. Each class and subclass defines a scope. Each scope is separate. To refer to variables in a different scope, you must refer to the fully scoped variable name. For instance, in the following example, we have a class and two subclasses with similar names defined within each of the classes:

```
class leader {
  notify {'Leader-1': }
}
class autobots {
    include leader
}
class autobots::leader {
  notify {'Optimus Prime': }
}
class decepticons {
  include leader
}
class decepticons::leader {
  notify {'Megatron': }
}
```

We then include the `leader`, `autobots`, and `decepticons` classes in our node, as follows:

```
include leader
include autobots
include decepticons
```

When we run Puppet, we see the following output:

```
t@mylaptop ~ $ puppet apply leaders.pp
Notice: Compiled catalog for mylaptop.example.net in environment
production in 0.03 seconds
Notice: Optimus Prime
Notice: /Stage[main]/Autobots::Leader/Notify[Optimus Prime]/message:
defined 'message' as 'Optimus Prime'
Notice: Leader-1
Notice: /Stage[main]/Leader/Notify[Leader-1]/message: defined 'message'
as 'Leader-1'
Notice: Megatron
Notice: /Stage[main]/Decepticons::Leader/Notify[Megatron]/message:
defined 'message' as 'Megatron'
Notice: Finished catalog run in 0.06 seconds
```

If this is the output that you expected, you can safely move on. If you are a little surprised, then read on. The problem here is the scope. Although we have a top scope class named `leader`, when we include `leader` from within the `autobots` and `decepticons` classes, the local scope is searched first. In both cases, a local match is found first and used. Instead of the three `'Leader-1'` notifications, we see only one `'Leader-1'`, one `'Megatron'`, and one `'Optimus Prime'`. If your normal procedure is to have the leader class defined and you forgot to do so, then you can end up being slightly confused. Consider the following modified example:

```
class leader {
  notify {'Leader-1': }
}
class autobots {
  include leader
}
include autobots
```

Now, when we apply this manifest, we see the following output:

```
t@mylaptop ~ $ puppet apply leaders2.pp
Notice: Compiled catalog for mylaptop.example.net in environment
production in 0.02 seconds
Notice: Leader-1
Notice: /Stage[main]/Leader/Notify[Leader-1]/message: defined 'message'
as 'Leader-1'
Notice: Finished catalog run in 0.04 seconds
```

Since the leader class was not available in the scope within the autobot class, the top scope leader class was used. Knowing how Puppet evaluates scope can save you time when your issues turn out to be namespace-related. This example is contrived. The usual situation where people run into this problem is when they have multiple modules organized in the same way. The problem manifests itself when you have many different modules with subclasses in different modules with the same names. For example, two modules named myappa and myappb with config subclasses, myappa::config and myappb::config. This problem occurs when the developer forgets to write the myappc::config subclass and there is a top scope config module available.

Metaparameters

Metaparameters are parameters that are used by Puppet to compile the catalog but are not used when modifying the target system. Some metaparameters, such as tag, are used to specify or mark resources. Other metaparameters, such as before, require, notify, and subscribe, are used to specify the order in which the resources should be applied to a node. When the catalog is compiled, the resources are evaluated based on their dependencies as opposed to how they are defined in the manifests. The order in which the resources are evaluated can be a little confusing for a person who is new to Puppet. A common paradigm when creating files is to create the containing directory before creating the resource. Consider the following code:

```
class apps {
  file {'/apps':
    ensure => 'directory',
    mode => '0755',
  }
}
class myapp {
  file {'/apps/myapp/config':
```

```
      content => 'on = true',
      mode => '0644',
    }
    file {'/apps/myapp':
      ensure => 'directory',
      mode => '0755',
    }
  }
  include myapp
  include apps
```

When we apply this manifest, even though the order of the resources is not correct in the manifest, the catalog applies correctly, as follows:

```
[root@trouble ~]# puppet apply order.pp
Notice: Compiled catalog for trouble.example.com in environment
production in 0.13 seconds
Notice: /Stage[main]/Apps/File[/apps]/ensure: created
Notice: /Stage[main]/Myapp/File[/apps/myapp]/ensure: created
Notice: /Stage[main]/Myapp/File[/apps/myapp/config]/ensure: defined
content as '{md5}1090eb22d3caa1a3efae39cdfbce5155'
Notice: Finished catalog run in 0.05 seconds
```

Recent versions of Puppet will automatically use the `require` metaparameter for certain resources. In the case of the preceding code, the `'/apps/myapp'` file has an implied require of the `'/apps'` file because directories autorequire their parents. We can safely rely on this autorequire mechanism but, when debugging, it is useful to know how to specify the resource order precisely. To ensure that the /apps directory exists before we try to create the /apps/myapp directory, we can use the require metaparameter to have the myapp directory require the /apps directory, as follows:

```
  classmyapp {
    file {'/apps/myapp/config':
      content => 'on = true',
      mode => '0644',
      require => File['/apps/myapp'],
    }
    file {'/apps/myapp':
      ensure => 'directory',
      mode => '0755',
      require => File['/apps'],
    }
  }
```

The preceding `require` lines specify that each of the file resources requires its parent directory.

Autorequires

Certain resource relationships are ubiquitous. When the relationship is implied, a mechanism was developed to reduce resource ordering errors. This mechanism is called **autorequire**. A list of autorequire relationships is given in the type reference documentation at `https://docs.puppetlabs.com/references/latest/type.html`.

When troubleshooting, you should know that the following autorequire relationships exist:

- A `cron` resource will autorequire the specified user. An `exec` resource will autorequire both the working directory of the `exec` as a `file` resource and the `user` as which the `exec` runs.
- A `file` resource will autorequire its owner and group.
- A mount will autorequire the mounts that it depends on (a mount resource of `/apps/myapp` will autorequire a mount resource of `/apps`).
- A `user` resource will autorequire its primary group.

Autorequire relationships only work when the resources within the relationship are specified within the catalog. If your catalog does not specify the required resources, then your catalog will fail if those resources are not found on the node. For instance, if you have a mount resource of `/apps/myapp` but the `/apps` directory or mount does not exist, then the mount resource will fail. If the `/apps` mount is specified, then the autorequire mechanism will ensure that the `/apps` mount is mounted before the `/apps/myapp` mount.

Explicit ordering

When you are trying to determine an error in the evaluation of your class, it can be helpful to use the chaining arrow syntax to force your resources to evaluate in the order that you specified. For instance, if you have an `exec` resource that is failing, you can create another `exec` resource that outputs the information used within your failing `exec`. For example, we have the following `exec` code:

```
file {'arrow':
  path => '/tmp/arrow',
  ensure => 'directory',
}
exec {'arrow_debug_before':
  command => 'echo debug_before',
  path => '/usr/bin:/bin',
}
```

```
exec {'arrow_example':
  command => 'echo arrow',
  path => '/usr/bin:/bin',
  require => File['arrow'],
}
exec {'arrow_debug_after':
  command => 'echo debug_after',
  path => '/usr/bin:/bin',
}
```

Now, when you apply this catalog, you will see that the `arrow_before` and `arrow_after` resources are not applied in the order that we were expecting:

```
[root@trouble ~]# puppet agent -t
Info: Retrieving pluginfacts
Info: Retrieving plugin
Info: Loading facts
Info: Caching catalog for trouble.example.com
Info: Applying configuration version '1431872398'
Notice: /Stage[main]/Main/Node[default]/Exec[arrow_debug_before]/returns:
executed successfully
Notice: /Stage[main]/Main/Node[default]/Exec[arrow_debug_after]/returns:
executed successfully
Notice: /Stage[main]/Main/Node[default]/File[arrow]/ensure: created
Notice: /Stage[main]/Main/Node[default]/Exec[arrow_example]/returns:
executed successfully
Notice: Finished catalog run in 0.23 seconds
```

To enforce the sequence that we were expecting, you can use the chaining arrow syntax, as follows:

```
exec {'arrow_debug_before':
  command => 'echo debug_before',
  path => '/usr/bin:/bin',
}->
exec {'arrow_example':
  command => 'echo arrow',
  path => '/usr/bin:/bin',
  require => File['arrow'],
}->
```

```
exec {'arrow_debug_after':
  command => 'echo debug_after',
  path => '/usr/bin:/bin',
}
```

Now, when we apply the agent this time, the order is what we expected:

```
[root@trouble ~]# puppet agent -t

Info: Retrieving pluginfacts

Info: Retrieving plugin

Info: Loading facts

Info: Caching catalog for trouble.example.com

Info: Applying configuration version '1431872778'

Notice: /Stage[main]/Main/Node[default]/Exec[arrow_debug_before]/returns:
executed successfully

Notice: /Stage[main]/Main/Node[default]/Exec[arrow_example]/returns:
executed successfully

Notice: /Stage[main]/Main/Node[default]/Exec[arrow_debug_after]/returns:
executed successfully

Notice: Finished catalog run in 0.23 seconds
```

A good way to use this sort of arrangement is to create an exec resource that outputs the environment information before your failing resource is applied. For example, you can create a class that runs a debug script and then use chaining arrows to have it applied before your failing resource. If your resource uses variables, then creating a notify that outputs the values of the variables can also help with debugging.

Defined types

Defined types are great for reducing the complexity and improving the readability of your code. However, they can lead to some interesting problems that may be difficult to diagnose.

In the following code, we create a defined type that creates a host entry:

```
define myhost ($short,$ip) {
  host {"$short":
    ip => $ip,
    host_aliases => [
      "$title.example.com",
```

```
        "$title.example.net",
        "$short"
    ],
  }
}
```

In this define, the namevar for the `host` resource is an argument of the `define`, the `$short` variable.

 In Puppet, there are two important attributes of any resource — the namevar and the title. The confusion lies in the fact that, sometimes, both of these attributes have the same value. Both values must be unique, but they are used differently. The title is used to uniquely identify the resource to the compiler and need not be related to the actual resource. The namevar uniquely identifies the resource to the agent after the catalog is compiled. The namevar is specific to each resource. For example, the namevar for a package is the package name and the namevar for a file is the full path to the file.

The problem with the preceding defined type is that you can end up with a duplicate resource that is difficult to find. The resource is defined within the defined type. So, when Puppet reports the duplicate definition, it will report it as though it were defined on the same line. Let's create the following node definition with two `myhost` resources:

```
node default {
  $short = "trb"
  myhost {'trouble': short => 'trb',ip => '192.168.50.1' }
  myhost {'tribble': short => "$short",ip => '192.168.50.2' }
}
```

Even though the two `myhost` resources have different titles, when we run Puppet, we see a duplicate definition, as follows:

```
[root@trouble~]# puppet agent -t

Info: Retrieving pluginfacts

Info: Retrieving plugin

Info: Loading facts

Error: Could not retrieve catalog from remote server: Error 400 on
SERVER: Duplicate declaration: Host[trb] is already declared in file /
etc/puppet/environments/production/modules/myhost/manifests/init.pp:5;
cannot redeclare at /etc/puppet/environments/production/modules/myhost/
manifests/init.pp:5 on node trouble.example.com
```

```
Warning: Not using cache on failed catalog

Error: Could not retrieve catalog; skipping run
```

Tracking down this issue can be difficult if we have several `myhost` definitions throughout the node definition.

To make this problem a lot easier to solve, we should use the `title` attribute of the defined type as the `title` attribute of the resources within the `define` method. The following rewrite shows this difference:

```
define myhost ($short,$ip) {
  host {"$title":
    ip => $ip,
    host_aliases => [
      "$title.example.com",
      "$title.example.net",
      "$short"
    ],
  }
}
```

Custom facts

When you define custom facts within your modules (in the `lib/facter` directory), they are automatically transferred to your node via the `pluginsync` method. The issue here is that the facts are synced to the same directory. So, if you created two facts with the same filename, then it can be difficult to determine which fact will be synced down to your node.

Facter is run at the beginning of a Puppet agent run. The results of Facter are used to compile the catalog. If any of your facts take longer than the configured timeout (`config_timeout` in the `[agent]` section of `puppet.conf`) in Puppet, then the agent run will fail. Instead of increasing this timeout, when designing your custom facts keep them simple enough so that they will take no longer than a few seconds to run.

You can debug Facter from the command line using the `-d` switch. To load custom facts that are synced from Puppet, add the `-p` option as well. If you are having trouble with the output of your fact, then you can also have the output formatted as a JSON document by adding the `-j` option. Combining all of these options, the following is a good starting point for the debugging of your Facter output:

```
[root@puppet ~]# facter -p -d -j |more
Found no suitable resolves of 1 for ec2_metadata
```

```
value for ec2_metadata is still nil
Found no suitable resolves of 1 for gce
value for gce is still nil
...
{
  "lsbminordistrelease": "6",
  "puppetversion": "3.7.5",
  "blockdevice_sda_vendor": "ATA",
  "ipaddress_lo": "127.0.0.1",
...
```

Having Facter output to a JSON file is helpful because the returned values are wrapped in quotes. So, any trailing spaces or control characters will be visible.

The easiest way to debug custom facts is to run them through Ruby directly. To run a custom fact through Ruby, start with the custom fact in the directory and use the `irb` command to run interactive Ruby, as follows:

```
[root@puppetfacter]# irb -r facter -r iptables_version.rb
irb(main):001:0> puts Facter.value("iptables_version")
1.4.7
=>nil
```

This displays the value of the `iptables_version` fact. From within IRB, you can check the code line-by-line to figure out your problem.

The preceding command was executed on a Linux host. Doing this on a Windows host is not so easy, but it is possible.

Locate the `irb` executable on your system. For the Puppet Enterprise installation, this should be in `C:\Program Files (x86)/Puppet Labs/Puppet Enterprise/sys/ruby/bin`. Run `irb` and then alter the `$LOAD_PATH` variable to add the path to `facter.rb` (the Facter library), as follows:

```
irb(main):001:0>$LOAD_PATH.push("C:/Program Files (x86)/Puppet Labs/Puppet Enterprise/facter/lib")
```

Now require the Facter library, as follows:

```
irb(main):002:0> require 'facter'
=>true
```

Finally, run `Facter.value` with the name of a fact, which is similar to what we did in the previous example:

```
irb(main):003:0>Facter.value("uptime")
=> "0:08 hours"
```

Pry

When debugging any Ruby code, using the Pry library will allow you to inspect the Ruby environment that is running at any breakpoint that you define. In the earlier `iptables_version` example, we could use the Pry library to inspect the calculation of the fact. To do so, modify the fact definition and comment out the `setcode` section (the breakpoint definition will not work within a `setcode` block). Then define a breakpoint by adding `binding.pry` to the fact at the point that you wish to inspect, as follows:

```
Facter.add(:iptables_version) do
confine :kernel => :linux
  #setcode do
version = Facter::Util::Resolution.exec('iptables --version')
if version
version.match(/\d+\.\d+\.\d+/).to_s
else
nil
end
binding.pry
  #end
end
```

Now run Ruby with the Pry and Facter libraries on the `iptables_version` fact definition, as follows:

```
root@mylaptop # ruby  -r pry -r facteriptables_version.rb


From: /var/lib/puppet/lib/facter/iptables_version.rb @ line 10 :


    5:      if version
    6:        version.match(/\d+\.\d+\.\d+/).to_s
    7:      else
    8:        nil
    9:      end
```

```
=> 10:    binding.pry
   11:    #end
   12:  end
```

This will cause the evaluation of the `iptables_version` fact to halt at the `binding.pry` line. We can then inspect the value of the version variable and execute the regular expression matching ourselves to verify that it is working correctly, as follows:

```
[1] pry(#<Facter::Util::Resolution>) > version
=> "iptables v1.4.21"
[2] pry(#<Facter::Util::Resolution>)>version.match(/\d+\.\d+\.\d+/).to_s
=> "1.4.21"
ok
```

Environment

When developing custom facts, it is useful to make your Ruby fact file executable and run the Ruby script from the command line. When you run custom facts from the command line, the environment variables defined in your current shell can affect how the fact is calculated. This can result in different values being returned for the fact when it is run through the Puppet agent. One of the most common variables that cause this sort of problem is JAVA_HOME. This can also be a problem when testing the `exec` resources. Environment variables and shell aliases will be available for `exec` when it is run interactively. When run through the agent, these customizations will not be available, which has the potential to cause inconsistency.

Files

Files are transferred between the master and the node via Puppet's internal fileserver. When working with files, it is important to remember that all the files that are served via Puppet are read into memory by the Puppet Server. Transferring large files via Puppet is inefficient. You should avoid transferring large and/or binary files. Most of the problems with files are related to path and URL syntax errors. The `source` parameter contains a URL with the following syntax:

```
source => "puppet:///path/to/file"
```

In the preceding syntax, the three slashes specify the beginning of the URL location and the Puppet Server that should be contacted. The following is also valid:

```
source => "puppet://myserver/path/to/file"
```

The path from which we can to download a file depends on the context of the manifest. If the manifest is found within the manifest directory or the manifest is the site.pp manifest, then the path to the file is relative to this location starting at the files subdirectory. If the manifest is found within a module, then the path should start with the modules path; then the files will be found within the files directory of the module.

Templates

ERB templates are written in Ruby. The current releases of Puppet also support EPP Puppet templates, which are written in Puppet. The debugging of ERB templates can be done by running the templates through Ruby. To simply check the syntax, use the following code:

```
$ erb -P -x -T '-' template.erb |ruby -c
Syntax OK
```

If your template does not pass the preceding test, then you know that your syntax is incorrect. The usual error type that you will see is as follows:

```
-:8: syntax error, unexpected end-of-input, expecting keyword_end
```

The problem with the preceding command is that the line number is in the evaluated code that is returned by the erb script, not the original file. When checking for the syntax error, you will have to inspect the intermediate code that is generated by the erb command.

Unfortunately, doing anything more than checking simple syntax is a problem. Although the ERB templates can be evaluated using the ERB library, the <%= block markers that are used in the Puppet ERB templates break the normal evaluation. The simplest way to evaluate Ruby templates is by creating a simple manifest with a file resource that applies the template. As an example, the resolv.conf template is shown in the following code:

```
# resolv.conf built by Puppet
domain<%= @domain %>
search<% searchdomains.each do |domain| -%>
```

```
<%= domain -%><% end -%><%= @domain %>
<% nameservers.each do |server| -%>
nameserver<%= server %>
<% end -%>
```

This template is then saved into a file named `template.erb`. We then create a file resource using this `template.erb` file, as shown in the following code:

```
$searchdomains = ['trouble.example.com','packt.example.com']
$nameservers = ['8.8.8.8','8.8.4.4']
$domains = 'example.com'

file {'/tmp/test':
content => template('/tmp/template.erb')
}
```

We then use `puppet apply` to apply this template and create the `/tmp/test` file, as follows:

```
$ puppet apply file.pp
```

Notice: Compiled catalog for mylaptop.example.net in environment production in 0.20 seconds

Notice: /Stage[main]/Main/File[/tmp/test]/ensure: defined content as '{md 5}4d1c547c40a27c06726ecaf784b99e84'

Notice: Finished catalog run in 0.04 seconds

The following are the contents of the `/tmp/test` file:

```
# resolv.conf built by Puppet
domainexample.net
search  trouble.example.com packt.example.com example.net
nameserver 8.8.8.8
nameserver 8.8.4.4
```

Debugging templates

Templates can also be used in debugging. You can create a file resource that uses a template that outputs all the defined variables and their values. You can include the following resource in your node definition:

```
file { "/tmp/puppet-debug.txt":
content =>inline_template("<% vars = scope.to_hash.reject { |k,v| !(
k.is_a?(String) &&v.is_a?(String) ) }; vars.sort.each do |k,v| %><%= k
%>=<%= v %>\n<% end %>"),
  }
```

This uses an inline template, which may make it slightly hard to read. The template loops through the output of the `scope` function and prints the values if the value is a string. Focusing only on the inner loop, this can be shown as follows:

```
vars = scope.to_hash.reject
{ |k,v| !( k.is_a?(String) &&
v.is_a?(String) ) };

vars.sort.each do |k,v|
k=v\n
end
```

Summary

In this chapter, we examined metaparameters and how to deal with resource ordering issues. We built custom facts and defines and discussed the issues that may arise when using them. We then moved on to templates and showed how to use templates as an aid in debugging. In the next chapter, we will work with Hiera and external node classifiers.

4

Hiera and External Node Classifiers

In this chapter, we'll cover how to deal with problems that may emerge while setting up and using Hiera. We'll also have a look at **external node classifiers** (**ENC**), which are used to apply classes to nodes. When problems arise, the ability to use Hiera and ENCs from the command line will allow you to quickly find where the errors have been introduced and which classes are being applied to your nodes.

Hiera is a great tool that reduces the complexity of your code by separating the data from the code and placing the data in a system where values are based on facts. Hiera is usually configured to use YAML files to look up values. In the next section, we'll examine some of the problems that are seen when using YAML files.

YAML files

In the great tradition of recursive acronyms, **YAML** expands to **YAML Ain't Markup Language**. YAML is a markup language that strives to be as human-readable as possible. The format is relatively simple. To signal the beginning of a YAML document within a file, use three dash characters (- - -). The end of the document is usually just interpreted as the end of the file in concern. However, you can specify the end of the document with three periods (. . .). Tokens are separated by colons (:). Most of the YAML code that you will encounter while working with Hiera will consist of *key:value* pairs.

Arrays are multiline elements, with each element of an array having its own line and a specific indentation. Indentation is important in YAML files in much the same way as it is in Python code. However, you can use square brackets ([]) or braces ({}) to represent an array on a single line.

Keys may only contain letters, numbers, and the underscore character. Keys must start with a letter.

Hiera is configured with a YAML file named `hiera.yaml`; this file may be in `/etc/puppetlabs/puppet`, `/etc/puppet`, or `/etc`. Hiera is currently written in Ruby and uses the Psych library to parse YAML files. Psych relies on LibYAML to parse the YAML files. For more information on Psych, visit the web page for this gem at `https://rubygems.org/gems/psych`, the gem page. For more information on LibYAML, visit the GitHub project page at `https://github.com/yaml/libyaml`.

When trying to diagnose YAML-related issues with Hiera, it's important to use the Psych and LibYAML libraries. An easy way to make sure that you are using these libraries is by writing a short Ruby script to parse files. The following script is one such example:

```ruby
#!/usr/bin/env ruby
require 'yaml'
require 'optparse'

# Add verbose option
options = {}
OptionParser.new do |opts|
opts.banner = "Usage: #{0} [options]"

opts.on("-v", "--verbose", "Verbose output") do |v|
options[:verbose] = v
end
end.parse!

# Loop through filenames given as arguments
for fn in ARGV
  if File.exists?(fn)
    begin
      testfile = YAML.load_file(fn)
      puts "YAML file (#{fn}) ok."
      puts testfile.to_yaml() if options[:verbose]
    rescue Psych::SyntaxError => p
      puts "YAML Syntax Error #{p.message}"
    rescue
      puts "Unspecified Error (#{fn})"
    end
  else
    puts "Error: File (#{fn}) not found.\n"
  end
end
```

This simple script will take the filenames for the YAML files as arguments and try to parse each of the files using Psych. Save this script as `yaml_check.rb` and make it executable, as follows:

```
$ chmod 755 yaml_check.rb
```

To test the script, create two YAML files. Create the first one with correct syntax and name it `correct.yaml`. The following are the contents of this file:

```
---
psych: is fun
ruby: too
```

Create a second YAML file named `incorrect.yaml` with incorrect syntax. The following are the contents of this file:

```
---
psych: works
ruby: should: too
```

Now, run the `yaml_check.rb` script against these two files to catch the syntax error in the second file, as follows:

```
t@mylaptop ~ $ ./yaml_check.rb incorrect.yaml correct.yaml
YAML Syntax Error (incorrect.yaml): mapping values are not allowed in
this context at line 3 column 13
YAML file (correct.yaml) ok.
```

The script was able to show where the syntax problem exists in the file. Such scripts can be useful if you wish to check your files before using them in production.

If you are using Git to update your hieradata files, you can add a similar script to your pre-commit Git hook to verify that only the valid YAML files are committed to your repository.

For more information on YAML, visit `http://yaml.org/`, the project website.

JSON

Although not commonly used as the primary backend for Hiera, **JavaScript Object Notation (JSON)** is also a backend option. JSON is generally not as readable as YAML. It is primarily meant to be easily parsed. An advantage of JSON is that it is widely used by web applications and can be easily generated. The JSON syntax can be verified using Node.js and the `JSON.parse` JavaScript function.

Consider the following JSON code, which is stored in the `example.json` file:

```
{ "books" : [
{ "title":"Mastering Puppet" , "pages":"300" },
{ "title":"Puppet Cookbook" , "pages":"250" },
{ "title":"Troubleshooting Puppet" , "pages":"100" }
  ]
}
```

We can parse the file with Node.js by using the `JSON.parse` function. Install the Node.js binary.

 Node.js is available at `https://nodejs.org/`. Node.js may be available via your system repositories. The package is named `nodejs` on most distributions.

Run `node`, as follows:

```
t@mylaptop ~ $ node
>varfs = require('fs');
undefined
>var file = fs.readFileSync('example.json','utf8');
undefined
>JSON.parse(file);
{ books:
[ { title: 'Mastering Puppet', pages: '300' },
{ title: 'Puppet Cookbook', pages: '250' },
{ title: 'Troubleshooting Puppet',
pages: '100' } ] }
>
```

We can wrap this up in a script like we did for YAML. Create the following Node.js script and name it `json_check.js`:

```
#!/usr/bin/env node

varargs = process.argv.slice(2);

varfs = require('fs');
for (vari = 0; i<args.length; i++) {
var file = fs.readFileSync(args[i],'utf8');
console.log(args[i],":");
console.log(JSON.parse(file));
```

You can then use this script to check the syntax of the `example.json` file from the command line, as follows:

```
t@mylaptop ~/trouble/03 $ ./json_check.js example.json
example.json :
{ books:
[ { title: 'Mastering Puppet', pages: '300' },
{ title: 'Puppet Cookbook', pages: '250' },
{ title: 'Troubleshooting Puppet', pages: '100' } ] }
```

Hiera

Hiera is great for the organization of the data that is used to deploy nodes. If you create a hierarchy that accurately describes your infrastructure, you can achieve great reductions in complexity. Debugging can be a pain, though. When debugging, you need to know the fact values that were used to retrieve the Hiera values. In this section, we'll work through an example of how a Hiera value can be changed, depending on the values returned by Facter.

For this example, we will configure Hiera with a custom hierarchy and then use the values from Facter on a node to perform lookups with the command-line Hiera tool:

1. Configure Hiera with the following hierarchy in `hiera.yaml`:

   ```
   :hierarchy:
     - defaults
     - hosts/"%{hostname}"
     - environments/"%{environment}"
     - architecture/"%{architecture}"
     - "%{operatingsystem}/%{operatingsystemrelease}"
     - global
   ```

2. Create hieradata files in the `architecture` and `operatingsystem` directories with values that we can retrieve, as follows:

   1. Create a YAML file in `architecture/x86_64.yaml`:

      ```
      ---
      bits: 64
      ```

   2. Create another YAML file in `RedHat/6.6.yaml`:

      ```
      ---
      release: "Nahant"
      ```

3. Next, add some values to `global.yaml`:

```
---
release: 'Tikanga'
bits: '32'
```

3. Use Hiera to look up the default value of `bits` without any Facter values, as follows:

```
[root@puppet ~]# hiera bits
32
```

4. Use the Facter values from the `trouble` node. To do this, log in to the `trouble` node and create a YAML file of the facts from that node, as follows:

```
[root@trouble ~]# facter -p -y >trouble.yaml
```

5. Next, copy the `trouble.yaml` file onto the Puppet master (or the machine where you've configured Hiera).

6. Use `trouble.yaml` as a reference when running Hiera, as follows:

```
[root@puppet ~]# hiera -y trouble.yaml bits
64
```

As you can see, by using the `trouble.yaml` file as a reference, the value returned by Hiera has changed from 32 to 64.

Supplying values to Hiera to perform lookups is useful for troubleshooting since you can change the Facter values to values that do not exist in your nodes, for instance, we could change the value of architecture to 128 and observe the output from Hiera. The other benefit of using the command-line tool is that it is possible, with the debug option, to view which of the hieradata files are searched in the hierarchy. As you will see in the next section, permissions for the files within the hierarchy are also important.

Permissions

As mentioned in the introduction, make sure that when you are debugging Hiera, you run all your tests as the `puppet` user. By default, the `puppet` user account is locked. I recommend running all your tests through `sudo`. Sudo is a tool that allows you to run commands as another user. It is similar to the `su` command (switch user), but it has fine-grained access controls that are configurable through the `/etc/sudoers` file (or files within the `/etc/sudoers.d` directory, depending on your version of `sudo`). As you will be using `sudo` from the root account, the default `sudoers` file will permit this access. If you are working in a production environment, you need to configure `sudo` to allow your personal account to run commands as the `puppet` user.

As shown in the following command, when you run the Hiera lookup through `sudo`, the `puppet` user does not have access to the `global.yaml` file. The Hiera lookup fails, as follows:

```
[root@puppet ~]# sudo -u puppet hiera bits
/usr/lib/ruby/site_ruby/1.8/hiera/filecache.rb:52:in 'read': Permission
denied - /etc/puppet/hieradata/master/global.yaml (Errno::EACCES)
    from /usr/lib/ruby/site_ruby/1.8/hiera/filecache.rb:52:in 'read_file'
    from /usr/lib/ruby/site_ruby/1.8/hiera/backend/yaml_backend.rb:17:in
'lookup'
    from /usr/lib/ruby/site_ruby/1.8/hiera/backend.rb:104:in
'datasourcefiles'
    from /usr/lib/ruby/site_ruby/1.8/hiera/backend.rb:76:in 'datasources'
    from /usr/lib/ruby/site_ruby/1.8/hiera/backend.rb:74:in 'map'
    from /usr/lib/ruby/site_ruby/1.8/hiera/backend.rb:74:in 'datasources'
    from /usr/lib/ruby/site_ruby/1.8/hiera/backend.rb:99:in
'datasourcefiles'
    from /usr/lib/ruby/site_ruby/1.8/hiera/backend/yaml_backend.rb:16:in
'lookup'
    from /usr/lib/ruby/site_ruby/1.8/hiera/backend.rb:206:in 'lookup'
    from /usr/lib/ruby/site_ruby/1.8/hiera/backend.rb:203:in 'each'
    from /usr/lib/ruby/site_ruby/1.8/hiera/backend.rb:203:in 'lookup'
    from /usr/lib/ruby/site_ruby/1.8/hiera.rb:60:in 'lookup'
    from /usr/bin/hiera:225
```

This type of error is common when you are not using some form of automation to update the files in the `hieradata` directory. Permission issues similarly occur for Puppet. The Puppet Server process runs as the `puppet` user as well (or `pe-puppet` for Puppet Enterprise).

PuppetDB

If your infrastructure is already configured for PuppetDB, you can pull the facts for a node using `puppet facts`, as follows:

```
[root@puppet ~]# puppet facts find trouble --render-as yaml>trouble-
puppetdb.yaml
```

You can then use this YAML file to look up the value of release:

```
[root@puppet ~]# hiera -y trouble-puppetdb.yaml release
Nahant
[root@puppet ~]# hiera release
Tikanga
```

PuppetDB automatically expires nodes. The expiry is returned in the output from `puppet facts find`. The key is the expiration, as follows:

```
[root@puppet ~]# grep expiration: trouble-puppetdb.yaml
expiration: 2015-03-31 02:03:37.672406 -04:00
```

If the output from `puppet facts find` is empty, your nodes have not checked into the master within the expiration period. This is a quick way to verify that the facts from your nodes are making their way into PuppetDB.

Debug

Hiera supports the debug option, which will output debugging information when looking up a value. Enable the debug option by appending `-d` as shown in the following command:

```
[root@puppet ~]# hiera -d release
DEBUG: Tue Mar 31 02:06:47 -0400 2015: Hiera YAML backend starting
DEBUG: Tue Mar 31 02:06:47 -0400 2015: Looking up release in YAML backend
DEBUG: Tue Mar 31 02:06:47 -0400 2015: Looking for data source global
DEBUG: Tue Mar 31 02:06:47 -0400 2015: Found release in global
Tikanga
```

As we suspected, the value from the `global.yaml` file was used to retrieve `Tikanga`. If we include the YAML file that we obtained earlier, we can see how it is used to retrieve `Nahant` from the `RedHat/6.6.yaml` file as shown in the following example:

```
[root@puppet ~]# hiera -d -y trouble-puppetdb.yaml release
DEBUG: Tue Mar 31 02:10:13 -0400 2015: Hiera YAML backend starting
DEBUG: Tue Mar 31 02:10:13 -0400 2015: Looking up release in YAML backend
DEBUG: Tue Mar 31 02:10:13 -0400 2015: Looking for data source hosts/
puppet
DEBUG: Tue Mar 31 02:10:13 -0400 2015: Cannot find datafile /etc/puppet/
hieradata/master/hosts/puppet.yaml, skipping
```

```
DEBUG: Tue Mar 31 02:10:13 -0400 2015: Looking for data source
architecture/x86_64
DEBUG: Tue Mar 31 02:10:13 -0400 2015: Looking for data source RedHat/6.6
DEBUG: Tue Mar 31 02:10:13 -0400 2015: Found release in RedHat/6.6
Nahant
```

Using the YAML facts file, Hiera was able to substitute the fact values into the hierarchy that we defined in /etc/hiera.yaml. Hiera then looked for the specific YAML files until it found the value in RedHat/6.6.yaml. By using these YAML files and the debug option, you can trace the path that was used to find the returned value.

strace

A common problem when debugging Hiera is mistakes in hiera.yaml. If you specify an incorrect directory or use a wrong variable name in your configuration, then Hiera will not find your YAML files. Using strace, you can intercept system calls. On a Linux system, when a program accesses files or opens network ports, it generally does so with library system calls. Each of these system calls, the arguments, and the return code will be written by strace.

 Each system call on Linux has its own manual page. You can issue man read or man open to look at the manual page for the read and open system calls. For example, the manual page for open shows that the return code for an open call is a file descriptor or -1 if the file failed to open.

When Hiera attempts to open YAML files, it must make a system call to open or read the file. We can have strace only report calls to the open system call. This is done with the -e trace=open option to strace. The syntax of running a command through strace is to type strace followed by the options to strace and then the command that you wish to run. To find out which files have been read by the hiera command, use the following construct:

```
[root@puppet ~]# strace -e trace=open hiera architecture 2>&1 |grep yaml
open("/etc/hiera.yaml", O_RDONLY)        = 3
open("/etc/puppet/hieradata/master/global.yaml", O_RDONLY) = 3
[root@puppet ~]# strace -e trace=open hiera -y trouble.yaml architecture
2>&1 |grep yaml\",
```

```
open("trouble.yaml", O_RDONLY)              = 3
open("/etc/hiera.yaml", O_RDONLY)           = 3
open("/etc/puppet/hieradata/master/architecture/x86_64.yaml", O_RDONLY) =
3
open("/etc/puppet/hieradata/master/global.yaml", O_RDONLY) = 3
```

In the preceding example, we can see that hiera only used the global.yaml file when we ran it without the trouble.yaml input file. After including the trouble.yaml file, hiera looked in both the architecture/x86_64.yaml and the global.yaml files while determining the value of architecture. Strace can help you debug many problems, not just Hiera.

> In the preceding command, we used the 2>&1 construct. This is used to redirect the error output from strace (STDERR) to STDOUT.
>
> Also, in the previous strace output, you will see that the file descriptor that was returned for each call to open was 3. We can then use this number to find the corresponding calls to the read function and inspect Hiera as it searches the files for the values.
>
> To do this yourself, run strace without the -e trace=open option and save the output. After a line containing open, look for the return value and find the next call to read with that number as the first argument.

puppet apply

Another way to debug Hiera is to use notify statements with puppet apply. This can be a lot quicker than running a full agent on a node when you need to look up a value. It also has the advantage of showing how Puppet will deal with the output of the lookup. The object returned by Hiera may be an array for instance. Consider a situation where we have the following in the global.yaml file:

```
---
release: 'Tikanga'
bits: '32'
clock:
  - 'one'
  - 'two'
  - 'three'
```

Then when we look up the value of `clock` with Hiera, we will see that an array is returned:

```
[root@puppet ~]# hiera clock
["one", "two", "three"]
```

However, when we run the following code through `puppet apply`, we see that the Puppet output is different. All the array values have been squashed into what appears to be a single string value:

```
[root@puppet ~]# puppet apply -e '$clock = hiera("clock") notify {
"clock=$clock": }'
Notice: Compiled catalog for puppet.example.com in environment production
in 0.05 seconds
Notice: clock=onetwothree
Notice: /Stage[main]/Main/Notify[clock=onetwothree]/message: defined
'message' as 'clock=onetwothree'
Notice: Finished catalog run in 0.11 seconds
```

Using `puppet apply` as shown in the preceding output, we can quickly investigate how Puppet will deal with the values returned by Hiera.

When using either `hiera_array` or `hiera_hash` on a key, be aware that these functions expect arrays in your YAML files. If your key has only a single value, then these functions will display an error, as follows:

```
[root@puppet ~]# puppet apply -e '$bits = hiera_array("bits") notify {
"bits=$bits": }'
Error: Could not run: Hiera type mismatch: expected Array and got Fixnum
```

Our earlier clock example was an array. So, using `hiera_array` on `clock` will return the results that we were expecting:

```
[root@puppet ~]# puppet apply -e '$clock = hiera_array("clock") notify {
"clock=$clock": }'
Notice: Compiled catalog for puppet.example.com in environment production
in 0.05 seconds
Notice: clock=onetwothree
Notice: /Stage[main]/Main/Notify[clock=onetwothree]/message: defined
'message' as 'clock=onetwothree'
Notice: Finished catalog run in 0.10 seconds
```

When Hiera is called with the normal `hiera` function, Hiera stops on the first match that is found. Using `hiera_array` will cause Hiera to continue finding values and return the results as an array.

The `hiera_hash` function will merge hashes. By default, if a hash key exists in multiple locations in the Hiera hierarchy, the first match will be used. However, you can change this behavior to a deep merge of the values; that is, each of the values is merged into the key for the returned hash. This option is specified in the `hiera.yaml` file with the following option in `hiera.yaml`:

```
:merge_behavior: deeper
```

Changing the value of `merge_behavior` and observing the results via the command-line utility is a useful troubleshooting tactic. In the next section, we'll see how to diagnose issues with external node classifiers.

External node classifiers – ENCs

ENCs are used to assign classes, parameters, and an environment to nodes. The output of an ENC must either be valid YAML or nothing. The simplest type of ENC is a script that is written using the `exec` node terminus, which executes the script that is pointed to by the `external_nodes` setting in `puppet.conf`.

When using the `exec` terminus, the exit code of the script should be zero, unless there is a problem executing the script.

When Puppet is configured to use an ENC, the output of the ENC is merged with the output from your `site.pp` file. This can be a problem when you are debugging. After a successful catalog compile and agent run, the `classes.txt` file will contain a list of all the classes that were applied to the node. The problem is that you may find it hard to determine whether the classes were found in `site.pp` or returned by the ENC.

ENCs can be written in any language. The only restriction on an ENC is that it accepts the hostname of a node as the first argument.

When debugging an ENC, it is important to make sure that the Puppet user can access the script. When the script is run, it will be run as the `puppet` user. When debugging, always run the script as the `puppet` user to verify that there is sufficient access to resources.

To debug your ENC, run the script as the puppet user, with your node's hostname as the primary argument. The ENC script is configured with the external_nodes option in the [main] or [master] section of your puppet.conf file. Check the value of this script and then run it with the name of your node, for example, trouble.example.com. For this example, I will use the simple_node_classifier script that I developed for *Mastering Puppet, Packt Publishing*.

1. Begin by creating the simple_node_classifier script in /usr/local/bin with the following contents:

```
#!/bin/env ruby

require 'yaml'

# create an empty hash
@enc = Hash.new
@enc["classes"] = Hash.new
@enc["classes"]["base"] = Hash.new
@enc["parameters"] = Hash.new
@enc["environment"] = 'production'

puts @enc.to_yaml
exit(0)
```

2. Place this script in the /usr/local/bin directory and ensure that it has the execute bit set and is readable by the Puppet user:

```
# chmod 755 /usr/local/bin/simple_node_classifier
```

3. Check the ENC settings in puppet.conf:

```
[main]
node_terminus = exec
external_nodes = /usr/local/bin/simple_node_classifier
```

4. Run the script as the puppet user with trouble.example.com as the first argument, as shown in the following command:

```
[root@puppet ~]# sudo -u puppet /usr/local/bin/simple_node_
classifier trouble.example.com
---

parameters: {}


classes:
base: {}


environment: production
```

When you run the Puppet agent on the `trouble` node, you will see that the class base was attached to the node. A useful construct when debugging is to update the ENC script to output the arguments to a file. This helps when nodes are checking in with a name or domain that is different from what you assume.

 The value of `certname` in `puppet.conf` can be used to specify a different name than the FQDN of a node when communicating with the master. The value of `certname` is stored in the top scope variable `$clientcert`.

Add the following code to the beginning of the `simple_node_classifier` script, directly after the `require 'yaml'` line:

```
#log the arguments
now = Time.new
log = File.open('/var/log/enc.log','a')
log.write("#{now.inspect}: #{$0}")
ARGV.each do |arg|
log.write " #{arg}"
end
log.write("\n")
log.close()
```

Now, try running the script and viewing the output of the log file that was created, as follows:

```
[root@puppet puppet]# /usr/local/bin/simple_node_classifier testing.
example.com
---
environment: production
parameters: {}

classes:
base: {}


[root@puppet puppet]# cat /var/log/enc.log
Thu Apr 02 01:08:01 -0400 2015: /usr/local/bin/simple_node_classifier
testing.example.com
```

Now go back to the `trouble` node and run `puppet agent` again to update the log:

```
[root@trouble ~]# puppet agent -t
Warning: Unable to fetch my node definition, but the agent run will
continue:
Warning: Find /production/node/trouble?transaction_uuid=c5d832f6-4927-
4392-8280-f3c1466f5d64&fail_on_404=true resulted in 404 with the message:
Not Found: Could not find node trouble
Info: Retrieving pluginfacts
Info: Retrieving plugin
Info: Loading facts
Error: Could not retrieve catalog from remote server: Error 400 on
SERVER: Could not find node 'trouble'; cannot compile
Warning: Not using cache on failed catalog
Error: Could not retrieve catalog; skipping run
```

Puppet failed. Something went wrong with our ENC. We ran the ENC as root initially. The log file was created with root as the owner. Puppet cannot write to the file. So, the script errors out. We can check the `puppetserver` logs on `puppetmaster` for this error:

```
2015-04-02 00:40:58,801 WARN  [c.p.p.ExecutionStubImpl] Executed an
external process which logged to STDERR: /usr/local/bin/simple_node_
classifier:6:in 'initialize': Permission denied - /var/log/enc.log
(Errno::EACCES)
    from /usr/local/bin/simple_node_classifier:6:in 'open'
    from /usr/local/bin/simple_node_classifier:6
```

To fix the problem, change the ownership on the log of the master:

```
[root@puppet puppet]# chownpuppet:puppet /var/log/enc.log
```

Then, go back to the `trouble` node and try the `puppet agent` run again:

```
[root@trouble ~]# puppet agent -t
Info: Retrieving pluginfacts
Info: Retrieving plugin
Info: Loading facts
Info: Caching catalog for trouble
Info: Applying configuration version '1427951625'
Notice: base class
```

```
Notice: /Stage[main]/Base/Notify[base class]/message: defined 'message'
as 'base class'
Notice: default node
Notice: /Stage[main]/Main/Node[default]/Notify[default node]/message:
defined 'message' as 'default node'
Notice: nothing
Notice: /Stage[main]/Main/Node[default]/Notify[nothing]/message: defined
'message' as 'nothing'
Notice: Finished catalog run in 0.05 seconds
```

Again, back on the Puppet master, use the `cat` command on the `enc.log` file:

```
[root@puppet puppet]# cat /var/log/enc.log
Thu Apr 02 01:08:01 -0400 2015: /usr/local/bin/simple_node_classifier
testing.example.com
Thu Apr 02 01:13:40 -0400 2015: /usr/local/bin/simple_node_classifier
trouble
```

As you can see, the output suggests that the `trouble` node does not have a fully qualified domain name. This might be a problem if our ENC uses domain names when classifying nodes.

The Foreman

The Foreman is a total automation solution, not just an ENC for Puppet. It can handle the entire lifecycle management for your nodes. You can use the Foreman to handle the configuration of your DHCP and DNS servers.

When using the Foreman as your ENC, the `node.rb` script will be installed in `/etc/puppet/node.rb`. This is a Ruby script that makes a REST call to the Foreman server. When your node first checks into the Puppet master, a record for the node is created in the Foreman. If you run `node.rb` on a host that has not yet been recorded by the Foreman, you will see the following error:

```
[root@foreman~]# /etc/puppet/node.rb trouble.example.com
No such file or directory - /var/lib/puppet/yaml/facts/trouble.example.
com.yaml
```

The preceding referenced YAML file is a cache file that Foreman creates after your node connects to it. After your node is connected to it, the following YAML file is returned when you run `node.rb`:

```
---
classes: {}
parameters:
puppetmaster: foreman.example.com
root_pw:
foreman_env: production
foreman_subnets: []
foreman_interfaces:
  - mac: 08:00:27:96:e0:fe
ip: 10.0.2.15
type: Interface
name:
attrs: {}
virtual: false
link: true
identifier: eth0
managed: true
subnet:
  - mac: 08:00:27:7c:fc:c6
ip: 192.168.50.101
type: Interface
name:
attrs:
mtu: '1500'
netmask: 255.255.255.0
network: 192.168.50.0
virtual: false
link: true
identifier: eth1
managed: false
subnet:
environment: production
```

If the webserver that is providing the REST service is unavailable, the cache file will be used. If the classes added through the Foreman GUI are not getting applied to your nodes, check these YAML files for the classes.

The Foreman has a **command-line interface (CLI)** known as `hammer`. With `hammer`, you can perform many management tasks for your nodes, such as adding and removing classes from nodes. For example, to list the available nodes in your Foreman installation, use the following command:

```
[root@foreman ~]# hammer host list
---|--------------------|----------------------|------------|-----------
|------------------
ID | NAME               | OPERATING SYSTEM     | HOST GROUP | IP
| MAC
---|--------------------|----------------------|------------|-----------
|------------------
1  | foreman.example.com | Springdale Linux 6.6 |            | 10.0.2.15
| 08:00:27:96:e0:fe
2  | trouble            | Springdale Linux 6.6 |            | 10.0.2.15
| 08:00:27:96:e0:fe
---|--------------------|----------------------|------------|-----------
|------------------
```

You can view the Puppet classes available, as follows:

```
[root@foreman modules]# hammer puppet-class list
---|---------------
ID | NAME
---|---------------
3  | base
1  | stdlib
2  | stdlib::stages
---|---------------
```

Using the preceding ID that was listed, you can add a class to a node, as follows:

```
[root@foreman ~]# hammer host update --name trouble --puppetclass-ids 3
Host updated
```

You can view the classes attached to the `trouble` node, as follows:

```
[root@foreman modules]# hammer host puppet-classes --name trouble
---|-----
ID | NAME
---|-----
3  | base
---|-----
```

Now when you run `node.rb` against the `trouble` node, you will see the base class:

```
[root@foreman ~]# /etc/puppet/node.rb trouble
---
classes:
base:
parameters:
puppetmaster: foreman.example.com
...
environment: production
```

The Foreman proxy

The Foreman communicates with the Puppet master via a proxy agent. This is to allow The Foreman and the Puppet master to be separate machines (or, as is usually the case, a cluster of machines). If you do not see your classes in the Foreman GUI, either the proxy isn't working or you haven't imported them yet. First, make sure that the service is running and listening on port 8443, as follows:

```
[root@foreman ~]# service foreman-proxy status
foreman-proxy (pid  2542) is running...
[root@foreman ~]# lsof -i :8443
COMMAND   PID          USER   FD   TYPE DEVICE SIZE/OFF NODE NAME
ruby     2542 foreman-proxy   5u   IPv4  31977      0t0  TCP *:pcsync-
https (LISTEN)
```

Then, go through the Foreman GUI and attempt to import your classes. Start by selecting **Puppet classes** from the **Configure** menu, as shown in the following screenshot:

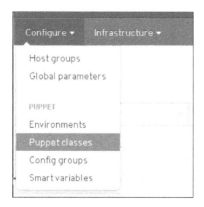

On the next screen, click on the import button:

Import from foreman.example.com

Finally, select the classes that you wish to import on the following screen. If the page fails to load at this point or you receive an error, the proxy is either not running or is inaccessible. The proxy has an API that you can query using `curl`. The API is documented at `http://projects.theforeman.org/projects/smart-proxy/wiki/API`.

To return `puppet` classes, the proxy has to support the `"puppet"` feature. To query the proxy to ensure that it supports the `"puppet"` feature, issue the following `curl` command:

```
[root@foreman ~]# curl --cert /var/lib/puppet/ssl/certs/foreman.example.
com.pem --key /var/lib/puppet/ssl/private_keys/foreman.example.com.pem
--insecure https://localhost:8443/features -H "Accept: application/json"

["puppet","puppetca","tftp"]
```

The preceding output indicates that this proxy supports the `puppet`, `puppetca`, and `tftp` features. If your Foreman GUI does not have the import button, then you will need to configure your smart proxies. The configuration of smart proxies is under the **Infrastructure** menu, as shown in the following screenshot:

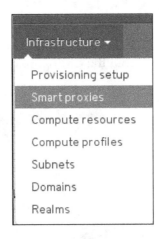

Most of the time, the Foreman works great and requires very little debugging. If you have a problem, the mailing list and the IRC channel, `#theforeman`, are good places to look for support. For more information on support for the Foreman, visit `http://theforeman.org/support.html`.

Puppet Enterprise

Puppet Enterprise (PE) has had a few different ENC implementations. Originally, the ENC for PE was a simple script that used `curl` to contact a REST API using the exec `node_terminus` (the script was named `external_node`). Version 3.2 included a new `node_terminus`, `console`. This change was made mainly for security reasons — to allow Puppet to ensure that the results from the `node_terminus` were genuine based on SSL certificates. With the release of PE 3.7, a new `node_terminus` was developed, which is far different from the first two iterations. This new terminus is called the node classifier. The classifier is configured by the `classifier.yaml` file in `/etc/puppetlabs/puppet`. This file specifies the host and port of the classifier. By default, this is `localhost` and port 4433. To interact with the classifier, you must use an SSL certificate that is on the whitelist located in `/etc/puppetlabs/console-services/rbac-certificate-whitelist`. The `pe-internal-dashboard` certificate is usually on this list. In my installation, the Puppet Enterprise server is `puppet.example.com`. To obtain information about `puppet.example.com` using the `pe-internal-dashboard` certificate, issue the following `curl` command:

```
[root@puppet ~] # curl --key /etc/puppetlabs/puppet/ssl/private_keys/pe-internal-dashboard.pem \

--cert /etc/puppetlabs/puppet/ssl/certs/pe-internal-dashboard.pem \

--cacert /etc/puppetlabs/puppet/ssl/certs/ca.pem \

-H "Content-Type: application/json" \

https://puppet.example.com:4433/classifier-api/v1/nodes/puppet.example.com>puppet.example.com.json
```

This will output a lot of data about the node. The classifier is a new way of defining which classes are applied to which nodes. It relies on inheritance and rules regarding which nodes should be included in which groupings. The classifier is more powerful than the previous ENCs. For more information on the API, visit `https://docs.puppetlabs.com/pe/latest/nc_index.html`.

For more information on the classifier itself, visit `https://docs.puppetlabs.com/pe/latest/console_classes_groups.html`.

LDAP

Another supported ENC for Puppet is LDAP. It is possible to store information about the Puppet node in the LDAP directory. When working with the LDAP node terminus, you can configure your Puppet Server to access the LDAP server in puppet.conf. The following settings are common:

```
[master]
node_terminus = ldap
ldapserver = ldap.example.com
ldapbase = dc=example,dc=com
```

Check whether Puppet can search the directory server by creating a simple Ruby script to search your directory for entries with the PuppetClient object class. Puppet will be using the same Ruby library. So, if this test fails, you know that Puppet will also fail. Create the following script in the ldapsearch-puppet.rb file:

```ruby
#!/usr/bin/ruby

require 'ldap'
Host = 'ldap.example.com'
Port = 389
base = 'ou=hosts,dc=example,dc=com'
scope = LDAP::LDAP_SCOPE_SUBTREE
filter = '(objectclass=PuppetClient)'
attrs = ['dn','puppetclass','puppetvar','environment']

c = LDAP::Conn.new(Host,Port)

begin
c.search(base,scope,filter,attrs) { |host|
putshost.dn
print "Classes: "
phost.vals('puppetclass')
  print "Variables: "
phost.vals('puppetvar')
  print "Environment: "
phost.vals('environment')
  puts "\n"
 }
rescue LDAP::ResultError
exit
end
```

Make the script executable and change the hostname, port, and base to match your environment. Run the script. If Ruby can communicate with your LDAP server, you should see the following output:

```
[thomas@puppet: ~] $ ./ldapsearch-puppet.rb

cn=puppet.example.com,ou=servers,ou=hosts,dc=example,dc=com

Classes: ["puppetmaster", "base"]

Variables: nil

Environment: production


cn=trouble,ou=hosts,dc=example,dc=com

Classes: ["base", "trouble", "logpolicy", "check_mk"]

Variables: nil

Environment: production
```

More information on the LDAP node terminus can be found at https://docs.puppetlabs.com/guides/ldap_nodes.html.

Summary

ENCs and Hiera are external tools that are used to manipulate the classes and the data that get applied to your nodes. Knowing how these tools work can help a lot when debugging. Knowing how your nodes are receiving classes makes it a lot simpler to remove classes that are causing problems. In the next chapter, we'll look at MCollective, a tool that is used to interact with nodes in real time.

5

The Marionette Collective

In this chapter, we will introduce the Marionette Collective (MCollective). We will have a look at the architecture of MCollective, which includes a message broker. We will examine the configuration of ActiveMQ, the preferred message broker for MCollective. We'll also learn how to diagnose issues with ActiveMQ. Then, we'll explore the MCollective command line utility, `mco`. Finally, we'll look at problems with time synchronization, network access, and logging.

Architecture

MCollective is the Puppet Labs orchestration engine. It is not just specific to Puppet and can be used alongside other configuration management systems such as Chef, Salt, and CFEngine. MCollective uses a message broker to facilitate communication between nodes. The preferred broker is ActiveMQ.

The various components of MCollective are outlined in the following diagram:

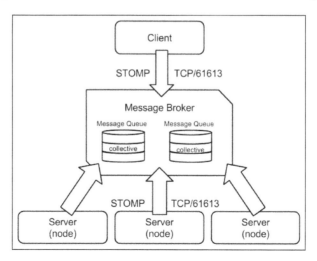

The important aspect of this structure is that when you query the collective, you don't query the nodes directly. The nodes are subscribed to a message queue, and you submit your query to the queue. Every subscribed node will receive the message. Each node will reply if it matches the selection criteria of the message. Otherwise, the node ignores the message.

Relying on a message broker has been a barrier to entry for most of the small shops, but using a broker solves a lot of scale-related problems. When you are debugging issues with MCollective, always start at the broker level.

Briefly, in MCollective terminology, every node that joins the collective runs the MCollective server, `mcollectived`. The configuration for this server is `/etc/mcollective/server.cfg`. When you query the collective for information, you use the `mco` client utility. The configuration for this utility is `/etc/mcollective/client.cfg`. Nodes connect to the broker via **Simple Text Oriented Messaging Protocol (STOMP)**. The great thing about STOMP is that you can check the connectivity by using tools such as telnet or Netcat. To verify your node can connect to the broker, check the following settings in the MCollective `server.cfg` file:

```
plugin.activemq.pool.1.host = puppet.example.com
plugin.activemq.pool.1.password = marionette
plugin.activemq.pool.1.port = 61613
plugin.activemq.pool.1.user = server
collectives = mcollective
connector = activemq
```

 The MCollective configuration files may be located in `/etc/mcollective` or `/etc/puppetlabs/mcollective`, depending on the version of Puppet that you are using.

From the code, we know that the hostname is `puppet.example.com` and the port is `61613`. We can attempt to contact the collective using Netcat, as follows:

```
[root@troublemcollective]# nc -v puppet.example.com 61613
Connection to 192.168.50.100 61613 port [tcp/*] succeeded!


CONNECT
login:server
passcode:marionette


^@
```

```
CONNECTED
heart-beat:0,0
session:ID:puppet.example.com-47411-1428904623350-2:13
server:ActiveMQ/5.9.1
version:1.0
```

If you do not have the username and password combination correct, you will see the following error:

```
ERROR
content-type:text/plain
message:User name [server] or password is invalid.


java.lang.SecurityException: User name [server] or password is invalid.
```

If this happens, check the username and password/passcode combination in the broker. If the Netcat session is unable to connect to the port, you need to check whether the broker is listening on the port locally. This can be done with lsof, a utility that lists open files. We can use the -i option of lsof to show only open network connections. We can then give the port number to show only the open connections for 61613, the port in question, as follows:

```
[root@puppet ~]# lsof -i :61613
COMMAND     PID      USER    FD    TYPE DEVICE SIZE/OFF NODE NAME
java       1016 activemq  118u   IPv6  12324      0t0  TCP *:61613 (LISTEN)
java       1016 activemq  119u   IPv6  12624      0t0  TCP puppet.example.
com:61613->puppet.example.com:54498 (ESTABLISHED)
java       1016 activemq  121u   IPv6  22073      0t0  TCP 10.0.2.15:61613-
>10.0.2.2:52052 (ESTABLISHED)
java       1016 activemq  122u   IPv6  22897      0t0  TCP
192.168.50.100:61613->192.168.50.1:45200 (ESTABLISHED)
mcollecti  1037      root    5u   IPv6  12623      0t0  TCP puppet.example.
com:54498->puppet.example.com:61613 (ESTABLISHED)
```

This output shows that there are nodes connected to port 61613. These connections are shown as ESTABLISHED. The important line in the preceding output is the first one. Your broker should be listening on the port, determined by LISTEN in the output. Even if you do not see any ESTABLISHED line, having the LISTEN line is enough to know that your broker is listening.

When connecting via Netcat, if the host is not listening, you will see a connection refused error message similar to the following:

```
[root@puppet ~]# nc -v localhost 61613
nc: connect to localhost port 61613 (tcp) failed: Connection refused
```

If your broker is not listening, you'll need to start troubleshooting the broker. In the next section, we'll look at the configuration of ActiveMQ (the broker suggested by Puppet Labs).

ActiveMQ configuration

ActiveMQ is an open source message broker. It is licensed by the Apache Foundation and is the recommended message broker for MCollective. ActiveMQ is configured by the `activemq.xml` configuration file (usually located in `/etc/activemq`).

It is possible that there may be a disconnect between your MCollective configuration and the ActiveMQ configuration. To check the port on which ActiveMQ is running the STOMP listener, look for the `transportConnector` line, which should look like this:

```
<transportConnector name="stomp+nio" uri="stomp://0.0.0.0:61613"/>
```

The **uniform resource identifier** (**URI**) specifies the connector that should be used. In the preceding line, the `0.0.0.0` address means that ActiveMQ will listen on all the interfaces and addresses on the server. For instance, if the address is `127.0.0.1`, then only local connections will be allowed, and you will not be able to connect to the broker from another machine. The port specified in the preceding line of code is `61613`. We expect a STOMP listener to respond to connections on this port.

After verifying that the broker is listening on the correct port, check whether the username and the password are correct. These will be set in a `simpleAuthenticationPlugin` stanza, as shown in the following code:

```
<plugins>
  <simpleAuthenticationPlugin>
    <users>
      <authenticationUser
        username="client"
        password="marionette"
        groups="servers,clients,everyone"
    />
          . . .
```

```
    </users>
  </simpleAuthenticationPlugin>
  ...
</plugins>
```

To use this user, the `client.cfg` file will need to have `client` as the username and `marionette` as the password. ActiveMQ grants authentication via maps. So, in order for the preceding account to be useful, we need an authentication map that grants access to the groups that have the `client` user as their member (servers, clients, and everyone):

```
<authorizationPlugin>
  <map>
    <authorizationMap>
    <authorizationEntries>
      <authorizationEntry queue="mcollective.>"
        write="clients" read="clients" admin="clients"
      />
      <authorizationEntry topic="mcollective.>"
        write="clients" read="clients" admin="clients"
      />
    </authorizationEntries>
          ...
    </authorizationMap>
  </map>
</authorizationPlugin>
```

The authorization entries in the preceding code grant the members of the `"clients"` group access to the MCollective queue. The `.>` syntax is a wildcard that provides access to all the subqueues under the MCollective queue.

If ActiveMQ is not running or unable to start up, the next place to look at is the log files. Logging is handled by the `log4j` Java logging package. Log4j is configured in the `log4j.properties` file. By default, log messages are sent to the file that is pointed at by the `log4j.appender.out.file` setting. For instance, if there is a syntax error in the `activemq.xml` configuration file, the error will be printed in the log file that is specified by the `log4j.appender.out.file` setting. On my test system, this log file was `/var/log/activemq/activemq.log`. After introducing a syntax error in the `activemq.xml` file, the following error is shown in this log:

```
org.springframework.beans.factory.xml.XmlBeanDefinitionStoreException:
Line 164 in XML document from class path resource [activemq.xml]
is invalid; nested exception is org.xml.sax.SAXParseException;
lineNumber: 164; columnNumber: 8; The element type "broker" must be
terminated by the matching end-tag "</broker>".
```

The ActiveMQ configuration file is written in XML. One of the quickest ways to find errors in XML is by running the file through `xmllint`. This program is a linter for XML and will output the same error that we saw in the log file, but with more context. It will make finding the problem much quicker. Here is the output from `xmllint`:

```
[root@puppetactivemq]# xmllint activemq.xml
activemq.xml:164: parser error : Opening and ending tag mismatch: broker
line 34 and end
</end>
       ^

activemq.xml:165: parser error : Opening and ending tag mismatch: beans
line 18 and broker
</broker>
         ^

activemq.xml:175: parser error : Extra content at the end of the document
</beans>
  ^
```

The problem that I introduced in the preceding output is that I added the closing clause, `</end>`, on line 164 of my configuration. The output from `xmllint` made this mistake much easier to find. Another option that can be used to debug XML is to load the file in your web browser. Opening the `activemq.xml` configuration file from Mozilla Firefox results in the error page, as shown in the following screenshot:

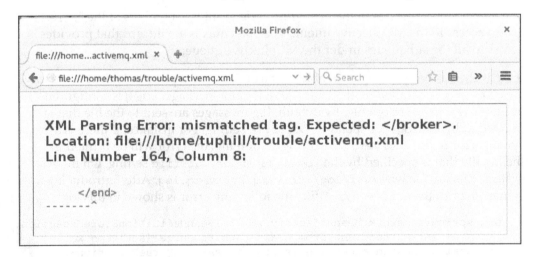

JMX

ActiveMQ is a Java process. When debugging a Java process, it helps to use the JMX management interface. This interface will give you an insight into the memory and CPU usage of the process. You can access the management interface through jconsole or VisualVM (for more information, visit https://visualvm.java.net/). To access the management interface, you will need to configure access, as outlined at http://activemq.apache.org/jmx.html. You can use jconsole locally without any configuration by running jconsole as the user configured to run ActiveMQ (on my system, this is the activemq user). If you start up jconsole without any options, the following connection selection dialog box will appear:

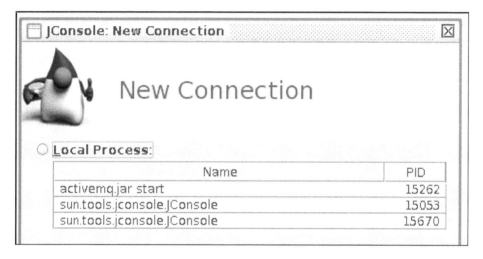

In the preceding screenshot, the ActiveMQ process has PID **15262**. Select it and click on **Connect**.

You can then view the CPU and memory usage of the process. To view the broker, click on the **MBeans** tab, navigate to org.java.activemq, and locate the broker, as shown in the following screenshot:

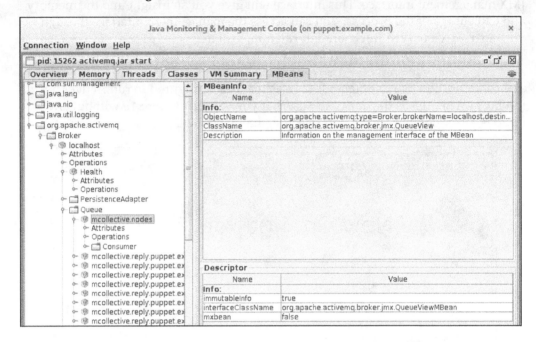

Additional ActiveMQ troubleshooting techniques can be found at http://activemq.apache.org/support.html.

ActiveMQ and resource limits

The ActiveMQ broker runs under the activemq user account by default. Most systems will limit non-root users' usage of resources using the user limit (ulimit) mechanism. When the broker runs as the activemq user, the number of open files permissible by the activemq user will limit the number of open connections that the process can have (each connection consumes an open file handle). Each node in the message queue needs an active connection. The number of nodes connected to the broker will be roughly equal to the number of open files allowed. After running a broker on my EL6 system, the default ulimit value is 1024, and the number of nodes that I would typically be able to reach via the broker is 1000. You can check the limit by running ulimit as the activemq user, as follows:

```
activemq@puppet $ ulimit -n
1024
```

The limit can be increased by creating a configuration file in `/etc/security/limits.d` or adding an entry to `/etc/security/limits.conf`. The syntax for these files can be found in the `limits.conf` manual page (using `man limits.conf`).

To change the number of open files that are allowed by the `activemq` user to `2048`, add the following to `/etc/security/limits.conf`:

```
activemq        soft    nofile          2048
activemq        hard    nofile          2048
```

If you are having trouble with limits, you may also wish to look at the **Pluggable Authentication Mechanism** (**PAM**) configuration for limits. The `pam_limits.so` library is used to configure the limits through PAM.

Using mco

To access your collective, you can use the API within Ruby or Python to create complex scripts. You can also use the `mco` command-line utility to perform simple queries and day-to-day tasks. In case something goes wrong with MCollective, `mco` is a good place to start if you want to troubleshoot it.

To check whether `mco` is configured properly and can access the collective, use `mco ping`, as follows:

```
[root@puppet ~]# mco ping
puppet.example.com                      time=89.71 ms
trouble.example.com                     time=129.69 ms


---- ping statistics ----
2 replies max: 129.69 min: 89.71 avg: 109.70
```

If you are unable to connect to the broker, you will see the following error:

```
[root@puppet ~]# mco ping


The ping application failed to run, use -v for full error backtrace
details: Received frame of type 'ERROR' expected 'MESSAGE'
```

As the output suggests, you need to pass the verbose flag to see the full error message:

```
[root@puppet ~]# mco ping -v

The ping application failed to run: Received frame of type 'ERROR'
expected 'MESSAGE'


Received frame of type 'ERROR' expected 'MESSAGE' (MCollective::Unexpecte
dMessageType)
        from /usr/lib/ruby/site_ruby/1.8/mcollective/connector/activemq.
rb:413:in 'receive'  <----
        from /usr/lib/ruby/site_ruby/1.8/mcollective/client.rb:122:in
'receive'
        from /usr/lib/ruby/site_ruby/1.8/mcollective/client.rb:244:in
'start_receiver'
        from /usr/lib/ruby/1.8/timeout.rb:67:in 'timeout'
        from /usr/lib/ruby/site_ruby/1.8/mcollective/client.rb:242:in
'start_receiver'
        from /usr/lib/ruby/site_ruby/1.8/mcollective/client.rb:197:in
'unthreaded_req'
        from /usr/lib/ruby/site_ruby/1.8/mcollective/client.rb:183:in 'req'
        from /usr/lib/ruby/site_ruby/1.8/mcollective/application/ping.
rb:57:in 'main'
        from /usr/lib/ruby/site_ruby/1.8/mcollective/application.rb:293:in
'run'
        from /usr/lib/ruby/site_ruby/1.8/mcollective/applications.rb:23:in
'run'
        from /usr/bin/mco:24
```

We can see the failed attempt to log in to the broker from the ActiveMQ log:

```
^@: org.apache.activemq.transport.stomp.ProtocolException: Not
connected.
2015-04-15 11:50:52,641 [calhost] Task-6] INFO  TransportConnection
- Stopping tcp://0:0:0:0:0:0:0:1:40872 because Failed with
SecurityException: User name [clien] or password is invalid.
```

The client is configured with the `mcollective/client.cfg` file. On versions prior to Puppet 4, this file is `/etc/mcollective/client.cfg`. In Puppet 4, this file has been moved to `/etc/puppetlabs/mcollective/client.cfg`. The format has not changed. For help troubleshooting the configuration, visit `https://docs.puppetlabs.com/mcollective/configure/client.html`.

Ping works, nothing else

When you troubleshoot `mco` problems, start with `mco` ping. All nodes will reply to a ping message. Most of the other `mco` plugins (facts, find, and RPC) rely on some sort of authentication mechanism to work. If you see many machines returned by the `mco ping` command but none or few with `mco find`, then you may have an authentication configuration problem. On my Fedora machine, the plugin is installed as a separate package, `mcollective-actionpolicy-auth`. The following lines in my minimal configuration file are used to configure the authentication:

```
rpcauthorization = 1
plugin.actionpolicy.allow_unconfigured = 1
rpcauthprovider = action_policy
```

When debugging, you can disable the authentication completely by having the following setting:

```
rpcauthorization = 0
```

Facts

One of the principal uses of MCollective is to perform an action on a subset of your nodes. You have two options to specify the nodes that you want—either by facts or by classes. For instance, in my troubleshooting installation, I have three nodes connected to the collective. One of these nodes is running Fedora. I can restrict my query to the Fedora machine by using the `operatingsystem` fact, as follows:

```
[root@trouble~]# mco find -v --wf operatingsystem=Fedora

Discovering hosts using the mc method for 2 second(s) ....1

mylaptop.example.com

Discovered 1 nodes in 2.01 seconds using the mc discovery plugin
```

How this works is important. The MCollective server process can be configured using one of two ways to handle facts. It can be configured to run `facter` each time it receives a message from the broker, but this can result in a long delay when running the MCollective commands. Alternatively, you can configure the server to reference a fact file. This is the default, but it's up to you to fill this file with the correct facts. Most of the installations will configure Puppet to update this file (`/etc/mcollective/facts.yaml` for Puppet 3 and `/etc/puppetlabs/mcollective/facts.yaml` for Puppet 4). If looking up nodes by facts is not working, then check this file. The default file only has a single fact:

```
---
mcollective: 1
```

To quickly populate this file, run `facter` as the Puppet or root user, as follows:

```
root@mylaptop # facter -p -y >facts.yaml
root@mylaptop # head facts.yaml
---
kernel: Linux
network_lo: "127.0.0.0"
network_vboxnet1: "192.168.50.0"
network_wlp3s0: "10.1.1.0"
lsbdistdescription: "Fedora release 21 (Twenty One)"
hostname: mylaptop
id: root
lsbdistcodename: TwentyOne
osfamily: RedHat
```

Discovery timeout

When you have a large number of nodes in your collective, you may need to extend the discovery timeout option when running the mco queries. If you find out that you are getting very inconsistent results when running mco, then the timeout option may help. The default timeout is 2 seconds. I've found out that 5 seconds is a better number in large installations. Using timeouts that are longer than 5 seconds doesn't appear to affect the results, and it makes the running of mco take too long (impatience is a virtue).

To set the discovery timeout to 5 seconds, add `--dt 5` to the command, as follows:

```
[root@trouble~]# mco find -v --dt 5
Discovering hosts using the mc method for 5 second(s) .... 2


trouble.example.com
puppet.example.com


Discovered 2 nodes in 5.01 seconds using the mc discovery plugin
```

Debugging and logging

Any `mco` command can be run with the `-v` (verbose) option. The verbose option outputs progress information as well as a summary. To debug `mco`, you have to edit the configuration file (`client.cfg`) and change the `loglevel` parameter. The default logging level is `warn`. Change this to `debug` when debugging. Another important option is `logger_type`. The `logger_type` option defines how `mco` outputs its logging information. The possible values are `syslog`, `file`, and `console`. With `loglevel` set to `debug`, you can trace the connection to ActiveMQ, as shown in the following output:

```
[root@trouble ~]# mco find -v
...
info 2015/04/17 17:59:35: activemq.rb:114:in 'on_connecting' TCP
Connection attempt 0 to stomp://client@puppet.example.com:61613
...
info 2015/04/17 17:59:35: activemq.rb:119:in 'on_connected' Connected to
stomp://client@puppet.example.com:61613
debug 2015/04/17 17:59:35: activemq.rb:437:in 'publish' Sending a
broadcast message to ActiveMQ target '/topic/mcollective.discovery.agent'
with headers '{"timestamp"=>"1429307975000", "expires"=>"1429308045000",
"reply-to"=>"/queue/mcollective.reply.trouble.example.com_5378.1", "mc_
sender"=>"trouble.example.com"}'
...
debug 2015/04/17 17:59:37: activemq.rb:460:in 'unsubscribe' Unsubscribing
from /queue/mcollective.reply.trouble.example.com_5378.1
...
info 2015/04/17 17:59:37: activemq.rb:124:in 'on_disconnect' Disconnected
from stomp://client@puppet.example.com:61613
```

If there were problems when connecting to ActiveMQ, they would be output in this debugging output. Combining this information with the logging information from the ActiveMQ broker makes the tracking down of problems quick.

Direct addressing

Both ActiveMQ and RabbitMQ (the supported middleware brokers for MCollective) support a mode that is known as **direct addressing**. Direct addressing means precisely what it sounds like. It is a mode where you define the nodes that you wish to contact without performing a discovery. You can directly communicate with the nodes by name. When working in a large environment, the ability to direct your queries to the correct machines without broadcasting them each time can help reduce the workload on your brokers and reduce network utilization. By default, direct addressing is on in the newer versions of MCollective and does not require any additional configuration. If it has been turned off, you can enable it with the following line in your configuration file:

```
direct_addressing = 1
```

You can enable direct addressing by either specifying a node source (text file, PuppetDB), or using the -I option for mco, as follows:

```
[root@puppet ~]# time mco facts architecture -I mylaptop
Report for fact: architecture


x86_64                                  found 1 times


Finished processing 1 / 1 hosts in 35.86 ms


real    0m0.247s
user    0m0.098s
sys     0m0.021s
```

As you can see, we did not have to wait the for the 2-second discovery time.

Time synchronization

The RPC commands that are sent by MCollective have **time-to-live** (**TTL**). After the TTL has expired, the messages are ignored by the clients and are removed from the queue by the broker. It is important to have the time on your machines synchronized. The TTL is given as the time when the message will expire. If the time on the node when creating the message is sufficiently ahead of the time on the receiving node, then the message will appear expired. If you have only a small number of nodes that are not replying to your queries, check whether the time synchronization is correct.

Summary

MCollective is a powerful orchestration tool. Most of the work in MCollective is done by the middleware broker. Almost all of the problems with MCollective come down to broker communication. Always start by checking whether your nodes can connect to the broker and they have the correct user information to connect.

In the next chapter, we'll look at two Puppet components that use the Puppet Labs TrapperKeeper framework. We'll see how to debug issues with these two components.

PuppetDB and Puppet Server

In the early days of Puppet, the only mechanism that could be used to store node data was a MySQL database. This database was used as the repository of external resources. This worked very well for small installations. When Puppet installations grew beyond small deployments of less than 1000 nodes, this mechanism broke down. The database couldn't keep up with the demands of all the nodes. A new system was developed that at first seemed quite complex, but it was mostly constructed out of necessity. The new system uses a web server to present a REST API. The REST API takes requests and sends them to a middleware message broker, which then routes the requests to a database. This new system is called PuppetDB. PuppetDB increased the number of nodes a single backend server could service from around 800 nodes to over 5000. The backend database server was changed from MySQL to PostgreSQL as well.

PuppetDB

PuppetDB presents a REST API on port 8080. The API allows you to query for node information. Connecting to the REST API is a good way to verify that the service is running, and contains good data. By using the REST API, you can query for facts, nodes, or reports. When PuppetDB is operating correctly, a query to the /v3/nodes/ URL will return a list of nodes in the database, as shown in the following command:

```
[root@puppet ~]# curl 'http://localhost:8080/v3/nodes'
[ {
  "name" : "puppet.example.com",
  "deactivated" : null,
  "catalog_timestamp" : "2015-05-04T15:01:09.628Z",
  "facts_timestamp" : "2015-05-04T15:01:06.469Z",
  "report_timestamp" : null
} ]
```

The REST API will always be available if PuppetDB is running. The HTTP API is available on port 8080, and the HTTPS/SSL API is available on port 8081. If PuppetDB is configured to run on your master, then the 8080 interface will be used. However, if PuppetDB is configured on a separate server, then the 8081 interface will be used, and you will need to ensure that your SSL certificates are accepted by the PuppetDB Server. To connect via the SSL API by using the local certificates, use the following command:

```
[root@puppet ~]# curl --cacert /var/lib/puppet/ssl/certs/ca.pem \
  --cert /var/lib/puppet/ssl/certs/puppet.example.com.pem \
  --key /var/lib/puppet/ssl/private_keys/puppet.example.com.pem \
  --tlsv1 https://puppet.example.com:8081/v3/nodes
[ {
  "name" : "puppet.example.com",
  "deactivated" : null,
  "catalog_timestamp" : "2015-05-04T15:01:09.628Z",
  "facts_timestamp" : "2015-05-04T15:01:06.469Z",
  "report_timestamp" : null
} ]
```

Querying the API either locally via HTTP or remotely via HTTPS is a good way to ensure that the service is running and accepting new data. If PuppetDB is not running, you will see errors that are similar to the following during puppet agent runs:

```
[root@puppet ~]# puppet agent -t
Warning: Unable to fetch my node definition, but the agent run will continue:
Warning: Error 400 on SERVER: Could not retrieve facts for puppet.
example.com: Failed to find facts from PuppetDB at puppet.example.
com:8081: Error executing http request
Info: Retrieving pluginfacts
Info: Retrieving plugin
Info: Loading facts
Error: Could not retrieve catalog from remote server: Error 400 on
SERVER: Failed to submit 'replace facts' command for puppet.example.com
to PuppetDB at puppet.example.com:8081: Error executing http request
Warning: Not using cache on failed catalog
Error: Could not retrieve catalog; skipping run
```

Internally, PuppetDB uses PostgreSQL as the backend storage for data. Previously, when MySQL was used, the schema was published and you could query the DB directly. With PuppetDB, the schema is private and you should not query the database directly. However, the PostgreSQL database can have issues, and knowing how to directly access this data will help you determine where your PuppetDB problem may be located.

The location of the database is configured in /etc/puppetdb/conf.d/database. ini. By using the username and password in this file, it should be possible to connect to the database and issue simple queries to ensure that the database is functional. For example, to connect to the PostgreSQL service that is running on the local machine, where the username is puppetdb, use the following command:

```
[root@puppet conf.d]# sudo -u puppetdb psql -W puppetdb
Password:
psql (8.4.20)
Type "help" for help.


puppetdb=> \dt
              List of relations
   Schema |          Name          |  Type  |  Owner
  --------+------------------------+--------+----------
   public | catalog_resources      | table  | puppetdb
   public | catalogs               | table  | puppetdb
   public | certnames              | table  | puppetdb
   public | edges                  | table  | puppetdb
   public | environments           | table  | puppetdb
   public | fact_paths             | table  | puppetdb
   public | fact_values            | table  | puppetdb
   public | facts                  | table  | puppetdb
   public | factsets               | table  | puppetdb
   public | latest_reports         | table  | puppetdb
   public | report_statuses        | table  | puppetdb
   public | reports                | table  | puppetdb
   public | resource_events        | table  | puppetdb
   public | resource_params        | table  | puppetdb
   public | resource_params_cache  | table  | puppetdb
```

```
 public | schema_migrations       | table | puppetdb
 public | value_types             | table | puppetdb
(17 rows)
```

To list the nodes in the database, execute the following query:

```
puppetdb=> SELECT * from certnames;
         name        | deactivated
---------------------+-------------
 puppet.example.com  |
(1 row)
```

This should be the same information that was returned by the API query.

Puppet Server

PuppetDB was widely adopted by Puppet installations. The success of PuppetDB led Puppet Labs to use the same architecture to improve the performance of the puppet master. A new Clojure-based framework called TrapperKeeper was developed. TrapperKeeper presents different services. For the Puppet master service, TrapperKeeper runs a JRuby process within a **Java Virtual Machine (JVM)**. This stack of components, with Clojure, JRuby, and Jetty, is also used by the new ENC solution of Puppet Labs, Puppet Node Manager. More information on the new node manager can be found at https://docs.puppetlabs.com/pe/latest/console_ classes_groups.html.

When run through Puppet Server, the Puppet master runs as a JRuby process within a JVM. The core Puppet code is stored in a JAR file named puppet-server-release. jar. The Clojure code is stored within this JAR file. JAR files are essentially ZIP archives. You can view the contents of the JAR file by using the ZIP utility, as follows:

```
[root@puppet ~]# unzip -l /usr/share/puppetserver/puppet-server-release.
jar |head
Archive:  /usr/share/puppetserver/puppet-server-release.jar
  Length      Date    Time    Name
---------  ---------- -----    ----
      137  03-28-2015 13:12    META-INF/MANIFEST.MF
     7597  03-28-2015 13:12    META-INF/maven/puppetlabs/puppetserver/pom.
xml
```

```
    5607   03-28-2015 13:12    META-INF/leiningen/puppetlabs/puppetserver/
project.clj

    5607   03-28-2015 13:12    project.clj

    3089   03-28-2015 13:12    META-INF/leiningen/puppetlabs/puppetserver/
README_BRANCHING.md

    5261   03-28-2015 13:12    META-INF/leiningen/puppetlabs/puppetserver/
README.md

   11325   03-28-2015 13:12    META-INF/leiningen/puppetlabs/puppetserver/
LICENSE.md
```

Alternatively, you can use the `jar` utility to view the contents of the JAR archive, as follows:

```
[root@puppet ~]# jar tf /usr/share/puppetserver/puppet-server-release.jar
|head

META-INF/MANIFEST.MF

META-INF/maven/puppetlabs/puppetserver/pom.xml

META-INF/leiningen/puppetlabs/puppetserver/project.clj

project.clj

META-INF/leiningen/puppetlabs/puppetserver/README_BRANCHING.md

META-INF/leiningen/puppetlabs/puppetserver/README.md

META-INF/leiningen/puppetlabs/puppetserver/LICENSE.md

META-INF/

META-INF/maven/

META-INF/maven/puppetlabs/
```

To debug Puppet-related problems, you will not need to know or decipher the Clojure files that were referenced in the previous section (such as `project.clj`). For `puppetserver`, the master service is what will bind to the masterport (8140) and answer the HTTP requests that arrive at the server. If you are having API issues or want to dive deeper into how requests are routed by the Clojure framework, unzip the master files from the JAR file and inspect them, as shown in the following output:

```
[root@puppet puppetserver]# unzip  puppet-server-release.jar puppetlabs/
services/master/master_core.clj puppetlabs/services/master/master_
service.clj

Archive:  puppet-server-release.jar
  inflating: puppetlabs/services/master/master_core.clj
  inflating: puppetlabs/services/master/master_service.clj
```

In these two files, you will see how the requests for API URLs, such as /node/*, are redirected to the appropriate handler:

```
[request-handler]
(compojure/routes
  (compojure/GET "/node/*" request
                 (request-handler request)))
```

For more information on Clojure, visit http://clojure.org/getting_started.

In the next section, we'll have a look at how one can debug the Ruby processes that run within the JVM.

Debugging Ruby

There are two supported ways to debug Ruby code with puppetserver — ruby-debug and Pry. Both of these will implement a **Read Eval Print Loop (REPL)**. A REPL allows you to type commands and have them evaluated in real time. When working with puppetserver, this gives you the power to inspect the puppetserver process while it is compiling a catalog or processing a report. Both ruby-debug and Pry are installed as Ruby gems. To use them with puppetserver, you have to install them by using the puppetserver gem command. I prefer to use Pry. So, I will show you how to use Pry in this example. We'll inspect calls to the hiera function by using Pry. To start, install Pry for use within puppetserver, as follows:

```
[root@puppet ~]# puppetserver gem install pry
Fetching: coderay-1.1.0.gem (100%)
Successfully installed coderay-1.1.0
Fetching: slop-3.6.0.gem (100%)
Successfully installed slop-3.6.0
Fetching: method_source-0.8.2.gem (100%)
Successfully installed method_source-0.8.2
Fetching: spoon-0.0.4.gem (100%)
Successfully installed spoon-0.0.4
Fetching: pry-0.10.1-java.gem (100%)
Successfully installed pry-0.10.1-java
5 gems installed
```

With Pry installed, we can modify the `hiera` function to include a binding to Pry within the definition of Hiera. This definition will be in the `hiera.rb` file within the `puppet/parser/functions` directory. On my test system, this is `/usr/lib/ruby/site_ruby/1.8/puppet/parser/functions/hiera.rb`. Modify the definition of Hiera within this file by adding the `require 'pry'` line, as follows:

```
HieraPuppet.lookup(key, default, self, override, :priority)
require 'pry'; binding.pry
```

Next, stop the `puppetserver` process and start it up again in the foreground. Puppet Server conveniently includes a foreground mode to facilitate this:

```
[root@puppet ~]# service puppetserver stop
Stopping puppetserver:                                    [  OK  ]
[root@puppet ~]# puppetserver foreground
```

Wait for the server to start. The `puppetserver` process will be ready to accept connections from agents once a message that is similar to the following is printed:

```
2015-04-22 04:52:23,519 INFO  [p.s.m.master-service] Puppet Server has
successfully started and is now ready to handle requests
```

With our Pry binding in place, we need to have a call to `hiera` in our catalog. Put the following in your `site.pp` file:

```
node default {
  $trouble = hiera('trouble','nothing to see here')
  notify {"$trouble": }
}
```

With this in place, start an agent run against `puppetserver`. This will start compiling the catalog until the compilation hits the call to `hiera`. At which point, `puppetserver` will print the following:

```
From: /usr/lib/ruby/site_ruby/1.8/puppet/parser/functions/hiera.rb @ line
33 #<Module:0x7b13e92c>#real_function_hiera:


    28:    More thorough examples of 'hiera' are available at:
    29:    <http://docs.puppetlabs.com/hiera/1/puppet.html#hiera-lookup-
functions>
    30:    ") do |*args|
    31:        key, default, override = HieraPuppet.parse_args(args)
    32:        HieraPuppet.lookup(key, default, self, override, :priority)
```

```
=> 33:    require 'pry'; binding.pry
   34:    end
   35: end
   36:
```

```
[1] pry(#<Puppet::Parser::Scope>)>
```

This is the Pry REPL shell. You can now type commands in this shell and have your commands evaluated in real time. In this instance, we can inspect the value of key, the key that is being looked up, as follows:

```
[1] pry(#<Puppet::Parser::Scope>)> puts key
puts key
trouble
=> nil
```

As expected, the value of key is trouble. The interesting thing is that we can alter the return value for the hiera call at this point by entering our own value, as follows:

```
[4] pry(#<Puppet::Parser::Scope>)> return "troubleshooting!"
return "troubleshooting!"
2015-04-22 05:10:12,226 INFO   [puppet-server] Puppet Compiled catalog for
trouble.example.com in environment production in 82.09 seconds
```

Back on the trouble node, we can see that the value that we entered previously is the value of notify:

```
Notice: troubleshooting!
Notice: /Stage[main]/Main/Node[default]/Notify[troubleshooting!]/message:
defined 'message' as 'troubleshooting!'
```

The ability to modify and inspect code while a catalog is compiling is very powerful. A word of caution here; to make the node apply the catalog successfully, you will need to exit the REPL shell before the node gives up and returns an execution expired error.

Debugging the core Puppet functions is a less common use of Pry. In practice, you would be debugging your own defined functions. If your custom function is synced with `pluginsync`, you can update the definition to include Pry when you send a special argument to your own custom function. As an example, consider a situation where the example function, `trouble`, has two arguments—a string and a debug flag, as shown in the following code:

```
module Puppet::Parser::Functions
  newfunction(:trouble) do |args|
    str = args[0]
    pry = args[1]
    if pry == true
      require 'pry'; binding.pry
    end
    puts "Trouble: #{str}\n"
  end
end
```

Create a module (`trouble`) and place the preceding code in a `trouble.rb` file within the `puppet/parser/functions` directory. Then, include a call to your new `trouble` function in your site manifest, as shown in the following code:

```
node default {
  trouble("nothing here")
}
```

Now, start a Puppet agent run. Note that the `nothing here` string is the output on the master:

```
2015-04-26 14:56:53,215 INFO  [puppet-server] Puppet Caching node for
trouble.example.com
Trouble: nothing here
```

Append a second argument to the preceding `trouble` function call, as follows:

```
node default {
  trouble("nothing here", true)
}
```

Now, when you start the agent again, you will be placed in a Pry shell. You can override the return value of the function as well:

```
From: /etc/puppet/environments/production/modules/base/lib/puppet/parser/
functions/trouble.rb @ line 6 #<Module:0x67b49977>#real_function_trouble:

    2: newfunction(:trouble) do |args|
    3:    str = args[0]
    4:    pry = args[1]
    5:    if pry == true
 => 6:      require 'pry'; binding.pry
    7:    end
    8:    puts "Trouble: #{str}\n"
    9: end


[1] pry(#<Puppet::Parser::Scope>)> puts pry
puts pry
true
=> nil
[2] pry(#<Puppet::Parser::Scope>)> puts str
puts str
nothing here
=> nil
[3] pry(#<Puppet::Parser::Scope>)> str="all good"
str="all good"
=> "all good"
[4] pry(#<Puppet::Parser::Scope>)> exit
exit
Trouble: all good
2015-04-26 14:59:40,997 INFO  [puppet-server] Puppet Compiled catalog for
trouble.example.com in environment production in 15.70 seconds
```

Running `puppetserver` in the foreground allows us to interact and interfere with the server in a way that was significantly more difficult to achieve with the Passenger implementation.

Puppet Server is configured from the /etc/puppetserver directory. The TrapperKeeper configuration file is bootstrap.cfg. Each line of this file contains the configuration of a service to start.

Logging

Puppet Server logging is handled by Logback. Logback is configured in the `logback.xml` file. The default level is INFO. This level can be increased to DEBUG by changing the line, as follows:

```
<logger name="org.eclipse.jetty" level="DEBUG"/>
```

After changing these settings, `puppetserver` will need to be restarted. The default location for the `puppetserver` log is `/var/log/puppetserver/puppetserver.log`.

 More information on Logback is available at `http://logback.qos.ch/`.

Both Puppet Server and PuppetDB use Logback for their logging configuration. As more Puppet applications are moved to the TrapperKeeper framework, they too will use Logback for logging.

Logging in the previous versions of Puppet, or when run without `puppetserver`, is configured in the `puppet.conf` configuration file. The configuration options for logging are the `logdir`, `masterlog`, and `log_level` options. The `log_level` option specifies which messages are written to the log. The available levels are `debug`, `info`, `notice`, `warning`, `err`, `alert`, `emerg`, `crit`, and `verbose`. After changing the value, you will need to restart the master, or the web server if you are running through Passenger.

Reports

When things go wrong, you rely on reports to keep you informed. After the agent completes the catalog application, if the agent is configured to send reports, it will assemble all the log messages that were generated during the catalog run as well as some metric information and compile this into a YAML object. The YAML object is returned to the master. By default, the master will dump the reports into files without any further processing, this is the `store` report type.

If the master is configured to run any other report processors (by setting multiple values for the `reports` setting in `puppet.conf`), then they will run in the specified order. The agent connection will remain open during this processing time and potentially return an error to the client. If the report processor does not complete within the timeout setting, then an `execution expired` error will be returned. The timeout can be tuned with the help of the `configtimeout` option in the `[agent]` section of `puppet.conf`.

This setting has been deprecated in favor of the `http_connect_timeout` and `http_read_timeout` settings. In Puppet 4, the `http_read_timeout` setting is unlimited. The types of timeouts that were previously seen should no longer occur.

Report processors are stored in the plugin report directory and are written in Ruby. The simplest report processor is the `store.rb` store processor. This simply stores the incoming YAML in a file. If you are writing your own processor, then this is the place to start. You can take the store report and modify it to suit your needs.

You can specify more than one processor in the `reports` setting. The processors are run in the specified order. If one of your processors is failing, to ensure that nothing is wrong with your configuration, place the `store` processor first in the list of reports and ensure that a report is being created in the `reports` directory on the master. Other report processors are available for having Puppet send reports to an IRC server or HipChat. Some of these processors are listed at `https://docs.puppetlabs.com/guides/reporting.html`.

PuppetDB can also be used to store reports. You will need to enable the PuppetDB report type to store reports in PuppetDB. One important thing to remember with reports is that they take up a lot of space and build up quickly. If you are using the store report type, then you need to arrange to remove the stale reports on a regular basis. A good thing about using PuppetDB is that the stale reports are removed automatically, by default, only 14 days of reports are retained.

In a large deployment, you may have a report only master configured. This is specified with the `report_server` directive in the `[agent]` section of `puppet.conf` on your agent nodes. For this type of configuration to work, your report master has to trust the certificate of the agent. The report master should use the same SSL certificate authority as your other Puppet master servers use.

Time

If you are using a separate `report_master`, then you need to be concerned about time. This is the same concern as when you have your certificate authority separate from your masters. The time must be synchronized to ensure that the certificate is valid. The validity period of a certificate is set when it is signed. The validity starts when the certificate is signed and by default, the period is 5 years. To view the validity, use the x509 utility of OpenSSL, as shown in the following command:

```
[root@puppet ~]# cd /var/lib/puppet/ssl
[root@puppet certs]# openssl x509 -in trouble.example.com.pem -text |grep -A2 Validity
```

```
Validity
    Not Before: Feb 28 06:30:00 2015 GMT
    Not After : Feb 28 06:30:00 2020 GMT
```

Time drift is a problem for many systems. Your systems should all synchronize their time to a central time source. If your systems drift (move away from true time) together, then it won't be a problem for certificates, only when you access external systems will this be a problem. When debugging, it is important to realize that the time of validity is contained within the certificate. If you have a multi-master configuration with your certificate authority is on a different machine, then you may run into a situation where nodes request certificates are signed by the CA but are not yet valid according to the time on your compile masters. The same situation happens when the time on your report master is behind that of the CA. This can be particularly confusing, as your node will apply the catalog but then fail to upload the report and return an error code for the Puppet agent run.

Time synchronization is important with SSL-protected services. When there are time synchronization issues, you will see errors such as the following:

```
Warning: SSL_connect SYSCALL returned=5 errno=0 state=SSLv3 read finished
A
```

When you connect to an SSL service using `curl` when there is a time synchronization issue, you will see the following type of error message:

```
curl: (60) Peer certificate cannot be authenticated with known CA
certificates
More details here: http://curl.haxx.se/docs/sslcerts.html
```

When using `curl` to debug this type of problem, you can add the `verbose` option to get more details. In this instance, we can see that the certificate has expired, as shown by the following error message:

```
* Remote Certificate has expired.
```

Summary

TrapperKeeper, Clojure, and JRuby are now the primary tools that are used to implement the Puppet services. As you've seen, you can debug these systems using the REST APIs that are provided by each service. The debugging of these services can now be handled in the same way as you would debug Java services.

7
Help Me!

In this chapter, we will explore the many places that you can turn to for help with regard to troubleshooting your problems, when you've exhausted your knowledge and the techniques provided in the previous chapters. The good thing about Puppet at the moment is that there are a lot of people using Puppet, and there is a lot of code out there that you can use as a reference.

Puppet Forge/GitHub

There are thousands of modules on Puppet Forge. Popular modules have not only been used in production in several locations, but have also been refined by several developers. When looking for a solution to your problem, the Forge modules can be a good starting point. Puppet Labs Supported and Puppet Labs Approved modules are excellent resources on how to write both code and comments.

When you can't find a solution to your coding problem, it is often useful to search the Forge for modules that may solve similar problems. The search feature of the Forge is not a deep search, and it is actually only useful if you wish to search for names or products. This isn't a problem though, since every module on the Forge is backed by a Git repository on GitHub. If you are just looking for code-related ideas, then search on `https://github.com/puppetlabs/`, the Puppet Labs page on GitHub. All the Approved and Supported modules have repositories at this location. When searching on GitHub, you can include the language for which you wish to get results. In our case, this will be Puppet, for example, to search for templates, try out the following search:

```
language:puppet template erb
```

By default, the best matches are shown first. When looking for code, the "most commented" option is usually a better search order.

Community help

To keep up with the general Puppet community announcements and ask questions, there is a Google Group set up at `https://groups.google.com/forum/#!forum/puppet-users`. The nice thing about this Google Group is that you can search through the previous posts for questions that are similar to your problem. There is also a Puppet Bugs forum. You can go through it by visiting `https://groups.google.com/forum/#!forum/puppet-bugs`, where JIRA tickets are discussed. You can also search the JIRA (the ticket system used by Puppet Labs, an Atlassian product) ticket database directly by visiting `https://tickets.puppetlabs.com`.

There is also a Puppet developers' group that is concerned with the Puppet language and its development. This group should not be used for general questions.

Puppet Labs also maintains a blog of updates and interesting Puppet articles. Reading the blog will also help you increase your Puppet awareness and possibly find new solutions to your problems. You can view the blog by visiting `https://puppetlabs.com/blog`.

Following some of the top Puppet Labs and Forge developers on Twitter is also a good way to stay up to date with what is going on with Puppet. The hashtag that you should search for is `#puppetize`, which avoids some ambiguity with the stuffed type of Puppet. You can also post a question with the `#puppetize` hashtag and see what replies you receive.

There is a small but active community on Reddit as well. If you post a question on `http://www.reddit.com/r/puppet`, you will certainly get an answer, or maybe even two.

IRC channels

There are two main channels devoted to Puppet, `#puppet` and `#puppet-dev`. The `#puppet` channel on freenode is an excellent forum if you wish to ask Puppet-related questions. However, it is assumed that you have read the available documentation, done some research on your own, and tried to solve your problem. Several of the Puppet Labs staff as well as community supporters are active in the channel and are willing to assist you in solving your problems. The `#puppet-dev` channel is reserved for discussions on the Puppet language and its implementation. Unless you have delved into the internal workings of Puppet, you will not need to consult this channel.

Both channels are logged and available at `http://www.puppetlogs.com/puppet/` and `http://www.puppetlogs.com/puppetdev`.

Puppet user groups

Puppet user groups (PUGs) are local social groups that get together, usually every month, to discuss their Puppet issues and share updates. There are several local PUGs. You can search for your local PUG by visiting `https://puppetlabs.com/community/PUG` on the Puppet Labs website. My local PUG is **PUGS (Puppet User Group of Seattle)**. Our website is `http://www.meetup.com/Seattle-Puppet-Meetup`. The format of the PUG meetings usually has a free form, but if you have encountered some problems, you will likely get a chance to ask for help. Often, a round of lightning talks will permit you to take the stage and state your problem to the group. In our group, this tactic has worked very well for some members; a problem that plagued them for days was solved quickly by the combined experience of the group.

Puppet Labs

When all else fails, you can contact Puppet Labs for a Professional Services engagement. Professional Services can be used to help design your workflow or help with your Puppet Enterprise installation. They can even help you write your own custom modules. More information on the services that are provided by Professional Services can be found at `https://puppetlabs.com/services/professional-services`.

Summary

Puppet has become a very popular configuration management tool. This is great news if you are having problems. There are a lot of other people who use Puppet and who can help you. Finding people who can help is a challenge. The ideas in this chapter should point you in the right direction so that you can get some traction while solving your issues.

If you still cannot find anyone who can solve your issues, I suggest broadening your search to include other configuration management tools such as Chef, Ansible, and Salt. If someone you know knows one of these tools and you can explain your problem, they may be able to help you phrase your problem correctly for a configuration management framework. Often, the problems that people have are more procedural in nature. They don't know how to do things in a system that is managed by a configuration management tool.

Index

explicit ordering
  defining 53-55
external node classifiers (ENCs)
  about 76-79
  Foreman 80-82
  LDAP 86, 87
  Puppet Enterprise (PE) 85

F

failed run 3
files 60, 61
firewalld
  reference 16
Foreman
  about 80-82
  proxy 83, 84
fully qualified domain name (FQDN) 6

G

Geppetto
  about 30-33
  URL 30
Google Group
  URL 120

H

Hiera
  about 69, 70
  debug option 72, 73
  permissions 70, 71
  puppet apply 74-76
  PuppetDB 71, 72
  strace 73, 74
hooks 46

I

Internet Systems Consortium (ISC)
    DNS server 27
iptables
  reference 16
IRC channels 120

J

Java Virtual Machine (JVM) 12, 108
jq
  about 13
  URL 13
JSON 67-69

L

last_run_report.yaml file 4
last_run_summary.yaml file 4
LDAP node terminus
  URL 87
**Lightweight Directory Access Protocol
    (LDAP)** 27
Logback
  about 115
  URL 115
logfiles 11
logging 101, 115

M

Marionette Collective (MCollective)
  about 89
  architecture 89-91
mco
  discovery timeout 100
  facts 99
  ping 99
  using 97-99
metaparameters
  defining 51, 52
modules
  defining 49

N

Name Service Switch (NSS) library 14
Netcat
  about 15
  URL 15
netgroups 28
Network File System (NFS) 28
Network Information Service (NIS) 27

O

Open Source Puppet (OSS) 18

P

Pluggable Authentication Mechanism
    (PAM) configuration 97
Professional Services
    URL 121
PUGS (Puppet User Group of Seattle) 121
Puppet
    about 49
    running 50, 51
puppet apply
    using 10
Puppet Bugs forum
    URL 120
Puppet code 25
Puppet configuration 4-6
PuppetDB 71, 72, 105-107
Puppet Enterprise (PE)
    about 18, 85
    URL 85
Puppet Forge 119
puppet help 7-9
Puppet infrastructure 1
Puppet Labs
    about 121
    URL 46
    URL, for blog 120
puppet-lint tool
    about 33-36
    URL 36
puppet master
    using 12
puppet parser validate
    using 11
puppet resource
    using 9
Puppet run
    lifecycle 2-4
puppetserver
    URL 12
    using 12

Puppet Server 108, 109
Puppet style guide
    URL 25
Puppet user groups (PUGs) 121

R

Read Eval Print Loop (REPL) 110
Reddit
    URL, for community 120
report processors
    about 115, 116
    URL 116
reports 115
resources.txt file 4
Ruby
    debugging 110-114

S

Simple Text Oriented Messaging Protocol
    (STOMP) 90
state.yaml file 4

T

templates
    about 61, 62
    debugging 62
time 116
time drift 117
time synchronization 103, 117
time-to-live (TTL) 103

U

uniform resource identifier (URI) 92

V

Vagrant
    about 39-45
    URL 45
Vim
    about 28
    URL 28
VisualVM
    URL 95

X

X509 certificates
  reference 23

Y

YAML files 65-67

Thank you for buying
Troubleshooting Puppet

About Packt Publishing

Packt, pronounced 'packed', published its first book, *Mastering phpMyAdmin for Effective MySQL Management*, in April 2004, and subsequently continued to specialize in publishing highly focused books on specific technologies and solutions.

Our books and publications share the experiences of your fellow IT professionals in adapting and customizing today's systems, applications, and frameworks. Our solution-based books give you the knowledge and power to customize the software and technologies you're using to get the job done. Packt books are more specific and less general than the IT books you have seen in the past. Our unique business model allows us to bring you more focused information, giving you more of what you need to know, and less of what you don't.

Packt is a modern yet unique publishing company that focuses on producing quality, cutting-edge books for communities of developers, administrators, and newbies alike. For more information, please visit our website at www.packtpub.com.

About Packt Open Source

In 2010, Packt launched two new brands, Packt Open Source and Packt Enterprise, in order to continue its focus on specialization. This book is part of the Packt Open Source brand, home to books published on software built around open source licenses, and offering information to anybody from advanced developers to budding web designers. The Open Source brand also runs Packt's Open Source Royalty Scheme, by which Packt gives a royalty to each open source project about whose software a book is sold.

Writing for Packt

We welcome all inquiries from people who are interested in authoring. Book proposals should be sent to author@packtpub.com. If your book idea is still at an early stage and you would like to discuss it first before writing a formal book proposal, then please contact us; one of our commissioning editors will get in touch with you.

We're not just looking for published authors; if you have strong technical skills but no writing experience, our experienced editors can help you develop a writing career, or simply get some additional reward for your expertise.

Mastering Puppet

ISBN: 978-1-78398-218-9   Paperback: 280 pages

Pull the strings of Puppet to configure enterprise-grade environments for performance optimization

1. Implement puppet in a medium to large installation.

2. Deal with issues found in larger deployments, such as scaling, and improving performance.

3. Step by step tutorial to utilize Puppet efficiently to have a fully functioning Puppet infrastructure in an enterprise- level environment.

Puppet 3 Cookbook

ISBN: 978-1-78216-976-5   Paperback: 274 pages

Build reliable, scalable, secure, and high-performance systems to fully utilize the power of cloud computing

1. Use Puppet 3 to take control of your servers and desktops, with detailed step-by-step instructions.

2. Covers all the popular tools and frameworks used with Puppet: Dashboard, Foreman, and more.

3. Teaches you how to extend Puppet with custom functions, types, and providers.

4. Packed with tips and inspiring ideas for using Puppet to automate server builds, deployments, and workflows.

Please check **www.PacktPub.com** for information on our titles

Extending Puppet

ISBN: 978-1-78398-144-1   Paperback: 328 pages

Design, manage, and deploy your Puppet architecture with the help of real-world scenarios

1. Plan, test, and execute your Puppet deployments.

2. Write reusable and maintainable Puppet code.

3. Handle challenges that might arise in upcoming versions of Puppet.

4. Explore the Puppet ecosystem in-depth, through a hands-on, example driven approach.

Puppet 3 Beginner's Guide

ISBN: 978-1-78216-124-0   Paperback: 204 pages

Start from scratch with the Puppet configuration management system, and learn how to fully utilize Puppet through simple, practical examples

1. Shows you step-by-step how to install Puppet and start managing your systems with simple examples.

2. Every aspect of Puppet is explained in detail so that you really understand what you're doing.

3. Gets you up and running immediately, from installation to using Puppet for practical tasks in a matter of minutes.

4. Written in a clear, friendly, jargon-free style which doesn't assume any previous knowledge and explains things in practical terms.

Please check **www.PacktPub.com** for information on our titles